ADVANCE PRA

Solar Light, Lunar Light
Perspectives in Human Consciousness

"The perception that masculine and feminine traits represent oppositional forces has contributed to a long history of personal and cultural dysfunctions. Through a skillful interweaving of modern psychology, mythology and ancient history, Howard Teich, PhD offers a thought provoking thesis that these polarizing traits are actually cooperative partners in evolution's dynamic dance. *Solar Light, Lunar Light* is a healing journey that encourages readers to transcend misperceived limitations so that we may write a new empowering chapter in human evolution."

> —Bruce H. Lipton, Ph.D., Cell biologist and bestselling author
> of *The Biology of Belief: Unleashing the Power of Consciousness,*
> *Matter and Miracles* and coauthor with Steve Bhaerman of
> *Spontaneous Evolution: Our Positive Future (And A Way To Get*
> *There From Here)*

"Howard Teich has discovered a brilliantly simple and invaluable way of helping men and women move towards wholeness and healing. With vivid examples from his therapeutic practice and from his own life, *Solar Light, Lunar Light* presents Teich's pioneering development of the solar/lunar polarity, and his sharp distinction of this from the masculine/feminine polarity with which it has long been uncritically and often destructively conflated. Recognizing this distinction, and moving towards a deep integration and rebalancing of the solar and lunar principles, represents a crucial task not only for every individual but for our civilization."

> —Richard Tarnas, Professor of Philosophy and Psychology,
> California Institute of Integral Studies, Author of
> *The Passion of the Western Mind* and *Cosmos and Psyche*

"Howard Teich has created a skillful and sensitive therapy based on the solar and lunar archetypes. His work is a fascinating enrichment of Jungian psychology that combines modern scientific theory with his own personal experience of emotional crisis. *Solar Light, Lunar Light* is a significant contribution to contemporary psychotherapy."
— Theodore Roszak, Professor emeritus of history at
California State University, Hayward. Author of
The Making of a Counter Culture and *The Voice of the Earth*

"*Solar Light, Lunar Light* is a daring and timely book that reconnects the human psyche to its natural roots. The result of an understanding of Dr. Teich's message cannot only offer personal transformation but, perhaps more significantly, may allow us to re-member how to live in balance within our interconnected world before it is too late."
— Four Arrows, aka Don Trent Jacobs, Ph.D., Ed.D., Author
of *Primal Awareness, Unlearning the Language of Conquest,
Critical Neurophilosophy* and *Last Song of the Whale*

Writing in *Solar Light, Lunar Light* about solar and lunar archetypes, "We could then put it simply that . . . every conscious event has both solar and lunar components."
— Fred Alan Wolf, Physicist, Writer and Lecturer on the
relationship of quantum physics to consciousness. Author of
eleven books. Recipient of the prestigious National Book Award
for *Taking the Quantum Leap*

"This book, by a practicing Jungian psychotherapist with long experience working with individuals who have taken the trouble to re-examine their relation to gender—what they can expect of themselves and their partners, friends, and co-workers—reflects years of careful reconsideration of what that task entails. He has exposed a basic flaw in the way we have all been taught, through the many waves of "enlightenment" that have made us think we were getting the jump in the race to master these issues before they master us. It is that we have not examined the light-source itself. We have tried, he reveals, to make ourselves conscious without considering the way the psyche itself approaches consciousness—which is both actively solar by day, when we discriminate, and reflectively lunar by night, when we dream. By showing us how to look at gender more naturally, through both of these lights, he makes us see facets of ourselves and our relations with others that our usual rational and romantic approaches, which are at best polarizing perspectives, have tended to miss. We can only be grateful even as we wonder why no one ever thought to write a book like this before."

—John Beebe, Jungian analyst, author of *Integrity in Depth*

"Howard Teich's book, *Solar Light, Lunar Light* is profound in the ways that it gives us to a deeper understanding of how we can find wholeness as individuals and how to develop a more balanced global community. In elucidating the archetypal meanings of solar and lunar consciousness, Teich helps us to move beyond limiting understandings of gender and what it means to be masculine or feminine as well as ways to value both solar and lunar ways of being and knowing. In our human history, we have shifted from a lunar way of being in prehistorical times to an idealization of solar ways in our historical, patriarchal period. Teich guides us on a path towards integration and the balance of these ways of consciousness that can be transformative for us individually and collectively."

—Heather Ensworth, Ph.D., clinical psychologist, astrologer and author of *Finding Our Center: Wisdom from the Stars and Planets in Time of Change.*

"This is a significant, life changing book. Howard Teich's work is crucial to understanding and healing the damage our rigid ideas of gender have done to us all, women and men alike. This is a book that can change how you see every problem you encounter and point you toward deeper more creative responses. Here is a psychology that has the potential of restoring us all and our world to wholeness."
—Susan Griffin, author of
A Chorus of Stones and *Woman and Nature*

"Teich has taken a core Jungian concept—the existence of a masculine and a feminine side of every person—and brought it (finally!) into the modern world. Instead of passive-receptive females and aggressive-dominant males, Teich brings us the lunar and solar sides of each of us, interacting in a delicate dance that is unique to each particular individual. This terminology, liberating us from the confines of sexual stereotypes, helps the reader to really see how constricting our old viewpoints are. Teich even offers us exercises that can help the reader identify where he or she is trapped and what steps can be taken toward a freer way-of-being. This book will open doors for every reader, helping each of us to find more of our true selves."
—Barbara Stevens

"Dr. Teich's lovely book makes a compelling and beautifully written case for the cultivation and practice of complementarity and phenomenological unity, ie. both/and consciousness, in our approaches to self and others, to gender and personality trait conflicts, and to cultural tendencies toward polarized reductionist thinking and behavior. Expanded awareness and the richness of living more whole peaceful lives with integrity are the clear results of moving beyond the gender and behavioral stereotypes with which we are so familiar. This book is a scholarly personal and loving contribution to us all in the journey to become more of who we are."
—Stephen J. Walsh, M.D., Clinical Professor of Psychiatry,
University of California San Francisco

SOLAR LIGHT, LUNAR LIGHT

PERSPECTIVES IN HUMAN CONSCIOUSNESS

SOLAR LIGHT, LUNAR LIGHT

PERSPECTIVES IN HUMAN CONSCIOUSNESS

HOWARD TEICH, PH.D.

GENOA HOUSE

Solar Light, Lunar Light
Perspectives in Human Consciousness

ISBN 978-1-926975-05-4 Paperback

Copyright © 2012 by Howard Teich
First Edition

Published simultaneously in Canada, the United Kingdom, and the United States of America. For information on obtaining permission for use of material from this work, please submit a written request to:
books@genoahouse.com

Genoa House
www.genoahouse.com

CONTENTS

To Dylan, a spirit of the future

ACKNOWLEDGMENTS

Thank you and deep gratitude to Susan Griffin, Springer Teich, Sara Teich, John Beebe M.D. and Kelly Peters for their love, support, and intellectual companionship on this long journey.

FOREWORD

The notion that two lights in the sky, the sun and the moon, have powerfully affected the way human beings have viewed their experience throughout most of human history is not new. However, we who live in a time that has acclimated to the prevalence and effects of artificial light have trouble recognizing this fact. We have lost the original sun and moon perspectives because we have so many other lights by which to "see." Indeed, we regard this from the standpoint of cognitive psychology as progress. Depth psychology, the persistent tradition of Freud and Jung, has offered a helpful counterweight to such Enlightenment optimism. We live by day and we dream by night, and these two worlds remain as different as they were in Ptolemy's day. But sadly we know that the earth revolves around the sun and that our definitions of masculinity and femininity, the subject of this book, have become too one-sidedly valuing of the traits associated with the solar. To speak metaphorically everyone today, it seems, would like their place in the sun; and we can barely see the moon for the artificial lights keeps our great cities glowing as symbols of opportunity for all. Readers will have to abandon their fluorescent imagination to get into the argument of this book which, though quite simple, may elude those who are unwilling to give up their cultural allegiance to the evolution of the notion of "superior" solar power. This book suggests that there is a lunar perspective, at least as important as the solar, to contribute to the accurate understanding of men and women. This can help correct conventional narrow "masculine" and "feminine" labeling of approaches to the living of life. In former times, people used solar and lunar to understand gender differences, but in different ways than we imagine today. We think solar has always implied masculine, and lunar feminine, and we imagine that we have freed humanity from the double bind of that binary which denies men who work a right to access their lunar sides, and women who care for their men at night any access to solar ascendancy in the world. We need to go further, and recognize that each gender has both solar and lunar attributes from the get-go, as part of our cultural birthright. The old myths do go further, with images like sun and water, which suggest this birthright is geological as well as, a condition for life itself on this planet. Older cultures once showed the way to reconnect with this "ultimate truth" by privileging twinship within each gender. Placing two men, or two women (twinning), side by side on the journey up the mountain to meet the father also provided them a chance to join each other below in the struggle to get past the barriers, or to reunite with an essential dark sister or brother in the underworld. Twinning is an archetypal structure in mythology. These two halves of men and women are seeking to unite in our own time, and in unity we will find the complementarity we are seeking and failing to find when we try to find it only in the other gender. I will take you on a tour of what I have gleaned from the cultural traditions that we have forgotten, and that only true scholars now know. I am a scholar of the heart and perhaps you are too—someone who can recognize a missing fragment and knows how to put it in its right place in the soul, if only someone will show you what it is. Let me show you what I have found . . .

INTRODUCTION

Solar Light, Lunar Light:
Perspectives in Human Consciousness

Three things cannot be long hidden: the sun, the moon, and the truth.
—Buddhist saying

There will be no peace in the battle of the sexes and no ecological sanity until we have finally done away with the nonsense of sorting human virtues into masculine and feminine bins.

—Ted Roszak

The Power of Light

Solar Light, Lunar Light is inspired by some of the first recorded symbols found in ancient rocks and bone carvings: the sun and the moon. Just as both the sun and the moon are crucial to the ecology of the planet, expressions of solar and lunar awareness in human consciousness are necessary for the well being of the soul.

Light has been associated with human awareness for thousands of years, since long before the beginning of recorded history. Light holds the power to heal souls. When we call a person with great wisdom and knowledge "enlightened," or refer to someone we think is crazy as "loony," we evoke a connection that has existed in almost all cultures for millennia. These metaphors draw their power from long human experience. The effects of brilliant sunlight or soft moonlight on the human psyche have been described by poets, transcending the boundaries of time and place. Using the metaphors for solar and lunar in our everyday language consciously aligns us energetically with these two primary lights of life.

The power that solar and lunar light and symbols have on human consciousness makes sense. We depend on light for photosynthesis to provide us with food, to create habitable environments, and to see the world around us. We are made of light. As electromagnetic sensory information, light is a signal from the environment which mysteriously translates into our inner awareness. How we perceive the world plays a crucial role in the life of our soul. "Soul," in the contemporary world, is borrowed from the ancient Greek word psyche. It is the root word of psychology and encompasses the modern idea of self and mind. Psychology is both what we see and the light we see it in, how we think, feel, live and, ultimately, who we are and is the prima materia of life.

Solar Light, Lunar Light is about a new approach to healing the soul. The light that enables us to see the world around us also shines within; there is a correspondence between our inner and outer worlds, and our place in those worlds. Ancient traditions from countless cultures have recorded and expressed this correspondence as a mirror of their reality. They used the source of light for our planet—the sun and the moon—as symbols for different aspects of the human psyche.

Myths and visual expressions depicting solar and lunar images have long claimed a central place in the human psyche, and have evolved from ordinary everyday experiences. Our ancestors used observation of the forces of nature as their explanation for how life worked. For example, the physical sun became a symbol of power and supremacy, just as following the phases of the moon was the source of counting and, eventually, mathematics. In addition, our sun is the source of all energy of life, and affects our emotions. On a bright sunlit day we are probably in a very different mood than on a cloudy one, or on a cool moonlit night. The ancient and universal deities reflect the difference between sunshine and moonlight, and the corresponding inner climate of the human soul. Deities with attributes such as strength, courage and clarity of vision have been associated with sunlight, and deities with attributes of emotional insight, sensuality and erotic powers have been associated with moonlight.

Biologist Dr. Bruce Lipton says, "evolution is an expansion of awareness." As humans, it would serve us well to cultivate the solar and the lunar sources of light within us. When we do, we are twice blessed. We have two modes of consciousness; two ways to know. In 1790, Du Pui wrote that we are *Homo duplex*, "double brain with double mind." Subsequent studies have shown the different modes of processing that occur in each of our brain's hemispheres. Numerous books have been written suggesting how to access one hemisphere over the other, with the emphasis on which side of the brain is being used. Although the solar and lunar hemispheres are connected in a single seamless perception of the world, they are unique in the specific types of information they process. Adopting a unified solar-lunar consciousness opens an awareness of not only a particular side being predominately used, but the awareness inherent in that orientation. We can consciously access information coming in, not just be subject to our ordinary patterning of one side or orientation over the other.

There is overwhelming neurobiological evidence that if we have a tendency to be more lunar, alpha brain waves (8 to 12 Hz) are more dominant; these manifest as visual, emotional and intuitive experiences. Beta brain waves (12 to 30 Hz) of the solar tendency manifest in language, ego, action and modes of execution. The other two major brain wave cycles of delta (1 to 4 Hz) and theta, (4 to 7 Hz) manifest in sleep and twilight sleeping states. This book will focus on the solar (beta) and lunar (alpha) brain cycles.

Solar and Lunar: The Two Modes of Consciousness

From the earliest recorded times to the present, the sun and its deities have symbolized a distinct group of human capacities. They include the ability to think clearly, to discern and judge, to calculate, and to follow a line of logic. The sun also symbolizes an aptitude to guide and lead, and to take decisive and effective action.

Solar figures were seldom depicted alone in the imagery we have of early cultures. Solar consciousness is not complete by itself. Throughout early human history solar deities have almost always been accompanied by lunar deities. The lunar deities represented a group of complementary, but different, human attributes such as the willingness to investigate reality through the senses, to know through emotions, to dream, and to receive insights intuitively.

To understand how these two aspects of consciousness affect daily life, imagine walking through a park in your neighborhood. In lunar mode, you might become aware of the feel of a slight breeze touching your cheek, then observe as it moves the leaves of a tree. You notice the sunlight as it streams through the tree to the ground. You might hear a bird singing or rustling in the underbrush, or see a squirrel as it darts up a tree and across a branch. Lunar consciousness allows you to appreciate the breadth of beauty and vitality, feeling a kindred spirit with these surroundings. The tranquility of the park seems to enter your body, to touch a place of deep quietude.

In solar mode, you might recognize different kinds of plants, be able to gauge the height of a tree or the girth of its trunk, notice signs of global warming, or identify the call of a songbird. Observations using solar consciousness are more active than receptive, and may, in fact, lead to action. For instance, you might notice that a section of the park is receiving too little irrigation and decide to alert the park service.

All of us possess both solar and lunar capacities. To be both logical and intuitive as well as strong and caring is a natural state of being. We have all inherited these age-old capabilities.

Solar and Lunar in Concert: The Conductor of Life Energies

Our thoughts, creativity, and personal relationships reach their full potential only when both solar and lunar aspects of the self are developed. When they are, these two sides work in concert. They guide us toward the decisions we need to survive and the perceptions we need to enjoy being alive. When one aspect of consciousness remains underdeveloped, we are likely to encounter serious problems and failures. Without emotional insight, for instance, logic easily becomes cold, if not merciless. Without the ability to analyze a situation, our emotions alone can deceive us, and lead us to chaotic or even disastrous consequences.

When the solar and lunar faculties work in harmony, they can produce a sum that is greater than their parts. Thought becomes more nuanced and richer when coupled with emotional insight. Cognitive scientists are discovering how empathy plays a crucial part in learning even the most analytical skills. Psychologists know that when emotions accompany clear insight, awareness deepens, moving more easily toward resolution and change. When we walk through the park, our scientific knowledge about the plants around us can increase our awe of them. The Naturalist John Muir often had deep, ecstatic experiences with nature because of his knowledge as a botanist. Yet, despite our powerful birthright of *twin consciousness*, many of us have developed the habit of favoring one mode of consciousness over the other from learned patterns.

Diminishing the full range of our innate human potential may be considered "normal" because we live in a culture that is out of balance. Western Judeo-Christian mythology and thinking has taken the innate complementarity of the two hemispheres and made the solar dominant over the lunar. For centuries, beginning with the earliest societies, survival depended on being able to outwit, outmaneuver, and physically overwhelm one's enemies. Our culture evolved to value the solar capacities of strength and dominance over the lunar capacities of relationship and empathy. In public roles we prefer leaders who are strong. To be emotionally intelligent or sensually aware is often misinterpreted as being weak and is, therefore, often considered a liability. People who have strong lunar qualities tend to not seek the spotlight. We have learned to polarize ourselves in ways that are unnatural.

The Way We Define Gender

The habit of denying our full range of human capacity has had a huge impact on the way we define gender. Nature has created solar-lunar patterns in which to live. We have taken those complementary patterns, forcibly delineated them, and stamped them with gender identification, and we have come to rely on cultural stereotypes to tell us what masculine and feminine are. This idea of substituting masculine and feminine distorts what nature shows us. Without questioning from where these assumptions derive, men are described as cerebral and assertive, and women as receptive and emotional. This view has become so entrenched that when we meet a man who expresses lunar qualities we may define him as being effeminate. A woman who expresses solar qualities is often referred to as being more masculine than feminine. These views do not reflect biology, but culture. It is our system of identifying sexuality by gender that produces suffering and alienation among those who do not match up to the cultural stereotypes.

Our current ideas of masculinity and femininity can be compared to the Procrustean bed. In this Greek myth, Procrustes was a robber who kept an inn by the road. His hospitality was more a curse than a blessing to travelers, however. The guests were required to fit exactly into their beds. If they were too short, Procrustes violently stretched them; if they were too tall, he chopped off their feet. Like Procrustes' guests, many men and women still find themselves force-fitted into the cultural bed of gender.

Gender stereotypes cause more harm than is evident on the surface. They affect those who are alienated from the conventional ideas of what it is to be masculine or feminine. When we identify with these views, we confine ourselves to the limitations inherent in the labeling. This confinement may lead to gender wounding. For example, a woman who adopts the cultural undertone may believe she lacks the capacity to do math or be assertive when she says, "I am a woman." Conversely, a man may believe that vulnerability or expressing tender feelings makes him less masculine when he states, "I am a man." These are mostly unconscious identifiers that have become embedded in our cultural definitions of gender. Countless men and women repress parts of themselves to fit in or avoid provoking prejudice. In so doing, they lose not only their ability to access those parts of themselves, but whole areas of consciousness from which those parts spring.

Most of us have repressed a significant part of ourselves in the name of cultural gender identity. To address the problems in our lives caused by society's definition of gender, we must first recognize that these definitions are false, but that alone is not enough. We have to rediscover, restore and develop those capacities we have learned to hide or ignore.

Reclaiming Our Birthright

Solar Light, Lunar Light is a tool for healing. It frees the psyche from rigid ideas about gender by using the broader, inclusive descriptive terms "solar" and "lunar" instead of the more limiting binary labels of "feminine" and "masculine," or right brain and left brain orientation.

Carl Jung was courageous and brilliant in his approach to the psychology of the unconscious mind, but he remained caught up in conventional categories of gender. This restricted his (and our) understanding of the genuine nature of the psyche. He realized that men and women shared traits, but described the different aspects of the human psyche as being either feminine or masculine. In other words, he defined men as having a feminine side and women as having a masculine side. With this logic he labeled the soul *anima*, a feminine foreign territory within a man's mind; and he labeled the spirit *animus*, a masculine foreign territory within a woman's mind.

Thus, instead of seeing the *lunar* masculine mode of consciousness (soul) as masculine for men, he continued to define men as having a feminine side. Instead of seeing women's *solar* mode of consciousness (spirit) as feminine, he saw women as having a masculine side, thereby continuing the gender mis-imprint placed by society. Jung, too, was a product of the artificiality of gender labeling that began with the Greco-Roman and Judeo-Christian definitions. He did not grasp that the qualities described belonged to both genders. Men and women have soul and spirit of their own gender; men have a solar and lunar masculine and women have a solar and lunar feminine. The duality of mind/body thinking is the root of many emotional conflicts in contemporary society not only between men and women, but between cultures as well. This viewpoint is so deeply entrenched into our worldview that most people don't understand that this can create a fragmented mind.

In summary, by calling the two aspects of human consciousness "lunar" and "solar," *Solar Light, Lunar Light* goes beyond the conventional categories of gender and the duality of thinking. The association of the moon with femininity and the sun with masculinity does not reflect the real properties of sunlight and moonlight. Prejudices

and misconceptions about gender that arose later in our history contribute to those associations. They began in Asia in about the third
or fourth century B.C.E. with the end of Taoism and the spread of
Confucian thinking, and in Western culture around 1,000 B.C.E. with
the rise of monotheism. The ancient cultures that gave birth to the
worship of solar and lunar deities included both lunar gods and solar
goddesses in their pantheons.

Just as the light of the sun and the moon (beta and alpha brain
waves respectively) falls upon all, solar-lunar consciousness belongs
equally to men and women. Just as the sun and the moon play complementary roles in nature, the solar and lunar modes of being are
co-creators in human consciousness. Co-creation is a concept that
postulates that we participate in the creation of reality rather than
creation only coming from a "higher" power or source outside us. By
claiming both aspects of our consciousness we reclaim a fullness of
being that is our birthright. With the restoration of both solar and
lunar modes of consciousness, we can recover dimensions of our
"selves" that have been lost.

This book describes how each of us can regain those lost parts of
ourselves. *Solar Light, Lunar Light* is a guide to seeing, to envisioning
through a new lens. The following chapters describe this approach
to integration and healing in more detail. Because *Solar Light, Lunar
Light* requires a radical shift of both heart and mind, I will describe
how my own thinking and life were changed by discovering the divi-
sion within myself. With that discovery, exciting possibilities for a
harmonious, well-balanced, and emotionally rich life became available to me.

CHAPTER ONE

Witnessing Light: My Story of Discovery

You must become an ignorant man again.
And see the sun again with an ignorant eye.
And see it clearly in the idea of it.

—Wallace Stevens

I like to think that the moon is there
even if I am not looking at it.

—Albert Einstein

Depression and Insight

I discovered the healing powers of light many years ago during my own journey through a pervasive and terrible depression, one I had suffered for years. One day, possessed by an especially dark mood, the image of a sunrise came to me. Light began to fill my imagination. I did not do anything to make this happen. As the day continued, and the "real" sun rose, I noticed my mood changing, becoming brighter and brighter. Though I did not fully comprehend it, by the time I went to bed that night, I was aware that something significant had happened. A long process of healing began and, thus, the start of an exploration which was to last many years and would become my life's work.

Although it would be a long time before I understood the meaning that this image of light had in my life, I was compelled to track down clues that might lead to its significance. I began by exploring the phenomenon of light itself. I became fascinated with photosynthesis: how, like plants and other animals, human beings are nourished by light. I studied the circadian rhythms of day and night and, eventually, the physics of light. I became aware of the extraordinary portrayals of light by different cultures throughout history.

A common theme reported by many who have experienced near-death encounters is feeling bathed in a brilliant light and the encompassing succor of universal love as they emerge from a dark tunnel or cave. My own experience with the "lightness of light" allowed me to understand, intuitively, why those who returned from such encounters reported that their experience of light led to profound transformation. The transformation from the darkness of the depression in which I lived, to the brilliance of the effect of that light I now experienced, was similar to the description of the profound shift described by near-death survivors.

In the mythologies of many cultures, the experience of light as a transformative force is repeated over and over again. *The Tibetan Book of the Dead* says that the soul is bathed in light after death. The Australian Wradjeri tells us about the shamanic initiate who experiences "the light man" after initiation; the Mexican shamanic candidate becomes "a light being." In the Western traditions of Judaism and Christianity, light is associated with primary creation: "And God said, 'Let there be light . . .'" Jesus, on whose life the Christian faith was created, said, "While I am in the world, I am the light of the world." (John 9:5)

All of these experiences of light from near-death encounters, initiations, and experiences of god are transformations, a form of rebirth for the person experiencing it. Just as birth is the process of developing from the void and emerging into the light, the experience of light is equally fundamental to the experience of rebirth. I had read about the concept of rebirth, but it seemed metaphysical and not real to me. My own spontaneous experience of light showed me that rebirth is another way of describing how new beginnings can come with an awareness of conscious insight. The knowledge that consciousness partners with enlightenment allows the freedom to know that when we can unhinge from the ways we have become attached to a mood or belief, we can evolve. This led to the insight that consciousness is often described as light, and its awakening is a form of rebirth. The light of being conscious is part of the rebirth of the soul.

When I awoke the morning after feeling enveloped by light, although outwardly I appeared in every way to be the same, inwardly, to the emotional core, and depth of my being, I was a different person. My understanding of this difference was vague, but I knew I would never be the same. The new personal significance of light, its expansiveness and impact on my life, pointed me on a journey to a new understanding of how to heal the soul.

My subsequent study of multi-cultural mythologies showed me the importance of light in creation, and in creating a person's sense of well-being.

However, there are actually two lights that cultures, mystics, and poets talk about, the sun and the moon. As we have become more industrialized and moved further from the natural world, we rarely consider our ancestor's reliance on the sun and moon as the most influential guides in their lives. In fact, as we have become modernized, the physical sun and moon have been replaced by metaphors in our language. The sun became referenced as male and the moon as female. But in earlier cultures, and even in intact indigenous cultures today, the sun was male *and* female just as the moon was also male *and* female. Although noting this labeling may seem inconsequential and even picky, the implications are profound. When we discover how these metaphors are buried in our cultural stories and language we can reconstruct some of the lost power of these primordial images and bring them back into our lives.

I am a man, and both culture and training taught me to think of myself as a solar being, just as women are trained to think of themselves as lunar souls. Yet after my encounter with light, I recognized that a crucial part of my "self" was missing. It was the lunar, symbolized by the moon, the complement to the solar and a fundamental aspect of a healthy mind and body. Being in touch with both the solar and lunar light within is what it means to be authentic.

To fully understand the magnitude of my eventual transformation, I will share some of my history. My initial experience was synchronistic, without premeditation or effort; it was a gift. But what I have learned can also be taught. It is a transformative, life-changing occurrence available to anyone who is willing to investigate the solar-lunar aspects of themselves.

Before I studied psychology and opened a private practice, I was employed as a buyer for a line of men's clothing. Even though I earned a good salary, I felt emotionally unsatisfied with the work. Looking back, I can see how I ended up in that career. Nothing in my childhood prepared me to explore what I really wanted from life. I came from a conventional 1950's family: my father worked, and my mother kept house and raised my brother and me. Like any American boy of that period, I was taught that the ideal American man was a solar hero: a Marine, a cowboy, a doctor or lawyer, even a baseball player. I was also programmed to get an education, marry, and become a family man. My parents however, added another damaging dynamic that shaped our family life. My father was a domineering man, emotionally withholding and harshly critical of the rest of us. He lacked empathy and demanded unquestioning obedience. Any show of independence threatened his solar identity and control. We never knew when he might lash out, or at whom, and for what infraction. My mother was a far more accessible, sympathetic person, but her tenderness had a shadow side. Dreamy and ineffective in the world, she relinquished her power to my father and allowed him to be emotionally abusive. As an adult, this strategy, although warped, became one way for her to survive in the relationship. As a parent however, her abdication of power allowed an abusive pattern to damage her children.

By the time I was a teenager, I began to understand my mother's situation and could empathize with her, but I did not want to fall into her pattern of submissiveness. I was determined to not be like my father, either. My mother's gentleness terrified me because I did not ever want to be mistreated as she was. So, in an unwitting defense against my father's tyranny, I repressed every vulnerable trait I associated with my dear, sweet, sad mother: kindness, warmth, tenderness, sympathy, gentleness—and resignation. I repressed my intuition and knowledge of my own inner life.

Following in my parents' footsteps and lacking any alternative models, I married a wonderful woman I hardly knew when I was twenty-four years old. We settled into a conventional life. My wife was also programmed to play the role of a good wife. During the next four years we caused each other a great deal of unhappiness. To try to save an unsuccessful marriage, we had a child, Sara, who brought enormous joy to both of our lives. However, with the exception of my daughter's birth and becoming a father, my life seemed in large part pointless. As I reached the goals I was taught to seek, I felt increasingly empty. All I could see ahead was more of the same charade. I was employed in a line of work that was meaningless to me. My life-long, low grade depression seriously escalated and by the age of twenty-eight, had become unmanageable.

Fortunately, in my despair, I decided to try psychotherapy. Early in the process, I did not get to the root cause of my suffering, but did begin to heal in other ways. Therapy enabled me to see and articulate that I was unhappy with my work and my personal life. I learned that by expressing my emotions I could restore a connection to my inner life, which was rich and flourishing, waiting to be recognized. No one had ever encouraged me to explore my real dreams and wishes, but now I became aware of ones I had ignored or forgotten. Uncharacteristically, I decided to take a risk and follow my intuition. Ignoring more practical considerations, I resolved to change professions. At that same time my marriage ended, and I began training to become a therapist.

It took three years to get my Ph.D. The year before I finished, I suffered a shattering blow. My mother committed suicide. I was stunned and shaken. The impetus for her suicide was the loss of her parents. Though they were both in their eighties and she was sixty-three, the level of her despair came as a shock to me.

My mother's suicide made me realize that emotionally she had still been a little girl. She had never accepted responsibility for her own life, instead depending on my father for day-to-day sustenance and on her parents for emotional succor. When they died, she was not only bereft, but adrift. Accepting this understanding was difficult, but it helped me to see that my own emotional life was still undeveloped.

Understanding a reality is not the same as feeling equipped to take action. For years after my mother's death I continued to be alienated from my feelings and intuitions, even as I was learning about them professionally. I was not able to fully mourn her death when it happened. The regression back to my earlier state began almost immediately after she died, as if an autopilot switch had been hit. I had been taught that a man's role in tragedy was to take charge and help others. I found myself efficiently managing details and helping my father and brother deal with their grief, but I did not experience my own.

My mother's death ended any fantasy I had of belonging to a "normal," loving family. I plunged even deeper into the well of darkness that had dominated my moods. My younger brother, Eugene, also suffered the effects of our mother's suicide. After much struggle, ten years later he also committed suicide. In the period between these two tragic events, the distrust I already felt toward others and toward my own feelings grew so large that I feared I would never have an intimate relationship. I was caught in a conflict of emotions, feeling both a great need for intimacy and at the same time not trusting that I was capable of achieving a loving relationship.

It may not come as a surprise that during this period, out of my loneliness and desire to prove I could be in an intimate relationship, I remarried. This union quickly failed, as did a series of other relationships. During this time while my work as a therapist was becoming successful and satisfying, I was still unhappy. I had, by now, personally been in therapy for almost two decades with various psychologists, but in the arena of love, I felt like a failure. Being professionally successful, even measured against my colleagues' definitions, made my personal life's failure even more confounding. Being a therapist and helping others has always been one of the greatest joys in my life, yet therapy was not healing me. This made me begin to question the value of the work itself.

Though I knew theoretically that therapy makes it possible to recover the authentic self, I sometimes felt more injured than the people I was helping to heal. No matter how hard I tried, I felt incomplete. Even my work to understand the kind of family dynamic that led to my mother's suicide did not heal my feelings of isolation. In retrospect, I can see that the causes of my depression were related not only to the past, but also to the cultural programming which had prevented me from experiencing the full range of myself in the present.

The Power of Integration

While I searched for what I felt was lacking, (which happens to many men who have a difficult time in relationships), my therapist, a Jungian analyst, suggested that the solution to my problem was to develop my feminine side.

Prior to psychoanalysis I had never heard of the concept of a feminine side within the male psyche. Taking my therapist's advice to heart, I looked for this mysterious aspect of myself. I read a great deal of psychological and spiritual literature in an effort to understand and develop what was called "the feminine side" of the masculine psyche.

As part of my research I became acquainted with C.G. Jung's ideas about the *anima* and *animus*. Jung believed that if we are to achieve wholeness, men need to integrate their feminine side (*anima*, or soul, in Latin) and women need to integrate their masculine side (*animus*, or spirit, in Latin). This integration occurs not only by having an intellectual understanding of the concepts, but in excavating these aspects which may be hidden in the psyche.

Though I tried to embrace the concept of the anima as the feminine side of me and incorporate it into my life, it still resulted in no significant change to me emotionally or in my relationship skills. Looking back, I can see that I was misguided by the labeling of the soul, the anima, as "feminine." In fact, the part of me that was lacking did resemble Jung's idea of the anima. However, in trying to develop my "feminine" side I had looked outside myself. I used the women I knew as models as I searched for a concrete definition of "feminine," and by so doing, overlooked the innate knowledge buried deep within me, waiting to be unearthed. There was something stirring in me, a deep knowledge buried within, but I did not know what it was yet. What I searched for and so desperately needed was my soul. I was to discover that this anima, mislabeled as feminine, was what I would eventually recover as part of my own nature as a man, as the lunar masculine.

If calling the emotional and intuitive side of the male psyche masculine instead of feminine seems like a trivial distinction, it is not. Symbolic changes cause major shifts in the realm of our personal psyches and our psychological approach to life. How we name and describe ourselves, and how we tell our stories, shapes our intellectual consciousness as well as our emotional lives. Only after making this subtle but significant shift in language, when I stopped calling my feelings "feminine" because they were in fact "masculine," was I able to recover what was missing in my life. These shifts allowed me to be open to discover that there is an emotional intuitive side in men that has nothing to do with the feminine, that is an aspect of deep masculine authenticity and integrity. The discovery of the lunar masculine and why it has been mislabeled feminine constitutes part of the rest of this story.

Twins

It was no coincidence that in the early darkness of my depression, long before I discovered the lunar masculine, that the archetype of light would start to reveal its healing power. I explored circadian rhythms, mythology, the physical nature of light, and went into Jungian analysis in a search to heal myself. My studies converged on an extraordinary image that eventually revealed concealed aspects of masculinity. In the last volume of the *Collected Works of C.G. Jung*, there are some strange pictures. One intriguing image, titled *The Revelation of the Hidden*, is of two men joined together in one body, like Siamese twins.

What could this bizarre image really mean? I knew on some level that this image held a key for me, but I was unable to make sense of it. Jung felt that alchemy was the key to understanding the psychology of the unconsciousness. He knew that in ancient days the alchemists focused on changing ordinary material into gold. The alchemists believed that they were working solely with physical matter. Jung realized that there was a corresponding transformation not only in the physical arena, but also in the psyche. The art of alchemy, long hidden, using secretive texts and images to avoid religious persecution, was now ready to be unveiled as a modern scientific tool in psychology. I felt that the bizarre alchemical image of the two men joined in one body might be relevant to me in some way, but wasn't sure how.

Then a synchronistic event occurred. Part of an answer to the mystery from the image of *The Revelation of the Hidden*, exposed itself to me at one particularly despairing time in those dark years. I went to see an immensely popular film called *Kiss of the Spider Woman*, for which William Hurt won an Academy award. Movies can be seen as a modern alchemical process that not only entertain us with their stories, but also teach about the courage and emotions necessary to psychologically address life. *Kiss of the Spider Woman* expanded my ideas of masculinity. The two heroes, Valentin, a macho revolutionary, and Molina, a homosexual window dresser desperately in love with romance, are very different—almost opposites. Yet circumstance has brought them together to share the same prison cell. To pass the time, Molina tells the story of Spider Woman. As he relates the plot with great drama, the two men get to know each other, become deeply bonded, and experience what it means to love, with each other. By the end of the story each has died the other's death: Molina, the romantic, is shot delivering a political message for Valentin; Valentin, the macho, is tortured to death while his mind is filled with romantic fantasy.

I was fascinated with this film and its implications. Because of their forced confinement together and the sharing of the story, they were finally able to see the other in his authenticity. This, in turn, opened the path to individual transformation, allowing each to incorporate the other's life through death. Love had transformed each of these men, allowing them to develop aspects they had neglected. Valentin became romantic, and Molina heroic. Power and tenderness combined were finally expressed within each individual; as they are meant to co-exist in each of us.

This movie reached me in a way that none of my prior reading or research ever had. I finally grasped some of the powerful meaning of *The Revelation of the Hidden*. I could see that tenderness as an aspect of masculinity was one of the hidden parts of the image, as it was also embodied in the movie. Power, the other of side of the masculine, was the yardstick used in our culture. But to measure masculinity without tenderness is incomplete.

I had a strong feeling that there were other questions that *The Revelation of the Hidden* and the film could answer as I tried to discover the link in what was still missing in my life. It was unclear to me from the movie why Spider Woman was the central figure in the title of the movie. I had a vague recollection that a figure called Spider Woman played a role in Navajo mythology, and soon discovered that, indeed, she was the mother of male twin heroes.

The concept of male twin heroes fascinated me. I knew about mythologist Joseph Campbell's famous book *The Hero with a Thousand Faces*, describing the hero archetype. Campbell alludes to twin heroes in this book, but has written little in depth about them. My newly directed quest to discover more about male twin mythology, however, led me to his first published work. The commentary, published five years before *The Hero with a Thousand Faces,* was included in Maud Oakes's *Where the Two Came to Their Father: A Navaho War Ceremonial.* Campbell's commentary describes Spider Woman's birth of the Navajo twins. Their destiny was to obtain the power weapons of the Sun Father to defeat a monster that was devouring their community. In looking at the many sand paintings that tell the story, I realized that this was a male initiation designed to teach the young twin spirits how to obtain the power to become adults. As part of the ritual they met the Sun Father in the house of the sun. Sun Father is accompanied by Moon Father, named Water Carrier. It was a surprise that Sun Father has a twin spirit, since the title of the ritual is "Where the Two Come to Their Father" not Fathers. Even in Navajo culture, a lunar twin is kept to the background of the story, used to highlight solar power. Both Sun Father and Water Carrier are needed to impart their power gifts to the twin initiates to carry out their destinies. The fathers test the twins with endurance challenges until they can obtain and control the resources within themselves, to handle the magnitude of the power of the weapons needed to defeat the monster. As in all initiation ceremonies, they are considered to have a "second birth" and given new names. One twin, who embodies the solar spirit, is called Monster Slayer, and given the color black in recognition of his power to deal with death. The other twin, embodying the lunar moon spirit, is called Child Born of the Water, and given the color blue in recognition of his power of birth and fertility.

With the discovery of the role of the twins in the Navajo culture, I could see that the two characters in the film were really mythic twins, spirit brothers who completed each other's nature. The Spider Woman in Navajo mythology gave birth to spirit brothers who complemented each other, just as Spider Woman in the filmed story allowed Molina and Valentin to complete their evolution and become spirit brothers. The male twin initiations were not only pertinent to a tribal mythology, but as the movie showed, able to have their lesson transcend time and culture.

Our consciousness determines how we see the world. I wondered how prevalent other twin heroes were in mythology. As I looked in the index of mythology books I was amazed. Male twin stories are found in the creation mythological structures of almost any culture recorded, in indigenous as well as in our own Western heritage. For example, male twins emerge in the Old Testament as Jacob and Esau, and in Christianity with Jesus and Thomas. Thomas, whose name literally means "twin," is Jesus' counterpart on earth. The Navajo twin initiates, hence, have a historical tradition of male twins to support them. The answer to my new area of inquiry into male twin mythology turned out to be the turning point of my adult life.

With the discovery of the prevalence of twin male mythology as the core of creation stories in so many diverse cultures, I remembered that story of the Roman twins Romulus and Remus is one of the founding creation myths in Western culture. However, Romulus and Remus was the only twin story I found that had a different ending than other twin myths. In other cultures, each male twin has a specific role which complements the other. In the story of Romulus and Remus, Remus is killed by Romulus. This mythological murder has profound significance to Western culture's psychology.

Cultural myths are vehicles for identity. As a dream often shows the complementary undeveloped part of an individual, a myth shows the complementary undeveloped part of a culture. I knew that I was closer to fully healing myself with this new information, but I was not there yet. I remembered that before I saw *Kiss of the Spider Woman* I was still depressed after so many years of analysis. Because of the two suicides in my immediate family, I began to think I might have a genetic defect and had little hope to ever heal myself. After discovering the omnipresence of the twin hero mythologies, I began to wonder if I could have a cultural, and not just a family or personal wound.

What did it really mean to see the world psychologically from a twin hero rather a single hero lens? What would it look like to view the world not from the solar hero archetype role described in *The Hero with a Thousand Faces* but from a twin solar **and** lunar consciousness depicted cross-culturally? Knowing I was so close to finding my answers made me feel more passionate and intensified my quest.

The Revelation of the Hidden

My persistent exploration of twin hero mythology kept drawing me back to Jung's alchemical picture of *The Revelation of the Hidden*. What did this have to do with contemporary male psychology? Aware now of twin rather than solo hero figures, I had an awakening flash of insight. I recalled that medieval alchemists disguised their secrets in obscure texts and metaphorical images for fear of reprisal from the church. Important alchemical messages were color-coded. The pictures I saw were reproduced in black and white, but the text describing them was printed in color. I realized that to capture the original illustration, I would have to color it in by hand. When I did this, using the written description as my guide, the legs that the Siamese twins shared were blue. So the color blue was the "revelation" that was hidden even in the alchemy tradition from those who practiced this art for personal gain rather than for societal and healing benefits. After this discovery of *The Revelation of the Hidden,* I remembered that one of the Navajo twins, "Child Born of the Water," was also blue and related to the male moon god "Water Carrier."

The answer for what I felt was lacking in me, that my first therapist set me on the search for, eventually came when I read about yet another male twin myth, this time coming from the Mayan culture. In this story, the gods of the underworld challenge a set of male twins to a battle. The mortal twins defeat the immortal gods, but in so doing, become aware that they are mortal and cannot defeat death. The twins jump into a fire to voluntarily die to their mortality and be reborn to immortality. When they emerge from the fire, one male twin is reborn as the sun, and the other male twin is reborn as the moon.

Finally the puzzle pieces came together for me. The lunar, the moon aspect I had always correlated to "feminine" was really masculine for men, and the Mayan myth was further evidence taken from one more, non-Western culture. Twin myths were both global and crossed time. It was the hidden piece in so many mythologies; present, yet obscured by the solar aspect so revered and used as the "moral" of the stories. Incorporating the power of the lunar aspect is as important a factor as incorporating the solar for men, just as the solar is as important a factor as the lunar for women. With this awareness, I felt my lifetime depression begin to lift.

The lunar masculine—portrayed as tenderness in *Kiss of the Spider Woman* was indeed the missing piece for my healing. What my therapist had earlier mistakenly labeled as my "feminine side" was this lost lunar twin. I realized that the lunar masculine is an archetype that exists in all men, regardless of their sexual orientation. I could see that each of the pair in *Kiss of the Spider Woman* was incomplete and out of balance. Valentin was harsh and unfeeling; Molina's overblown emotions made him seem silly. I wondered how these men's lives would be different if they each realized that twin masculinity is the core architecture of being a man. This included being both a physical and an emotional warrior. What would have happened if they had developed the other's aspects that were missing in themselves? What if Valentin had made love more of a priority in his life? If Molina could fight for what he believed? Each man in this pair completed the other. The realization of their complementariness was deeply satisfying.

After the discovery that there is a lunar aspect of the masculine, I went back to other cultures that had twin hero myths and found that solar and lunar archetypes were omnipresent. This validated my insight that the existence of the lunar side of masculinity had been killed in Western culture. Male moon gods existed with the solar as a universal mythos.

Solar and lunar twins have many manifestations and types of relationships. Some exist peacefully and cooperatively, others are antagonistic. In indigenous cultures I have not yet come across a myth where one male twin is killed by the other. The two exist in a complementary relationship, representing both sides of masculinity in balance. One brother is a physical warrior, a goal-directed and logical aspect of the psyche; the other shows the spiritual, process-oriented, emotional and intuitive aspect.

From this emerging picture I saw that lunar attributes—the capacities for emotional intelligence, sensual knowledge, intuition and imagination—are not just feminine descriptions, they are also masculine. Belonging to both, in other words, they are human. Conversely, the capacity to lead and think analytically does not belong exclusively to men but, quite naturally, to women also. Consciousness is not gender specific. The prison depicted in *Kiss of the Spider Woman* is symbolic of the prison that restricts both men and women.

Accepting lunar qualities as masculine, I was able to recognize and then develop them in myself. I always had a sensual, emotional and intuitive side which I had repressed. I had been embarrassed or ashamed of my emotions. As I learned to reveal my feelings instead of hiding them, I was able to approach my problems and those of my clients more creatively. I had gained access to the deepest recesses of myself. Like an eternal flame, it had, and has, never gone out.

Now I understood why I had been so wounded as a man. The twin authentic nature of masculinity (power and tenderness) has been distorted to create a false ideal of masculinity (power alone). I had not only my personal family's dysfunctional issues with which to contend but, like every man brought up in Western culture, I had a cultural wound that needed to be healed. This wound was created when Romulus usurped and destroyed Remus. Remus, the lunar male twin, was killed for power, for religious and political reasons. Growing up in a culture that murdered the lunar masculine forced me to kill off those same instincts as they emerged in me. Thus, calling the lunar masculine "feminine" was not just a personal issue, it has become, as later chapters will illustrate, a cultural tragedy culminating in worldwide issues.

The archetype of twin heroes emerges as part of the collective unconscious. The collective unconscious is a reservoir of the human experience built on cooperation and symmetry, as well as discord and the valorization of dominance. The repression of the twin archetype has significant consequence for all of us. As a society, we have suffered from the exaggeration of some traits and the diminution of others. In a world where aggression is more evident than empathy, and competition more frequent than cooperation, the balance of the lunar side of the human psyche is sorely needed.

Reorienting to the understanding that masculinity has both solar and lunar aspects, I saw that coupled solar and lunar structures exist in mythology involving women too. It is not found as twins, but in the relationships between mother and daughter, sisters, companions, and even in mothers-in-law and daughters-in-law. Examples include Demeter and Persephone (mother and daughter), Echo and Hera (from the myth of Narcissus), and the sisters Inanna and Ereshkigal.

To only tell one mythological story of the feminine does not do justice to the magnitude of the cost to women of the repression of the solar feminine in Western Culture. The myth of Inanna and Ereshkigal is representative, however, of the tragedy of Western Culture's disdain of the solar feminine in how a woman relates to herself, to other women, and to men. There is a profound price paid in the evolving selfhood for women, as there was for me as a man. Culture can repress an archetype, but it cannot kill it. The archetype will return with a vengeance and burst forth with renewed strength. The return of the authentic solar and lunar feminine is becoming apparent in women's personal lives as well as in politics and business. The examples in the remainder of the book show the value of the rebirth of the solar and lunar to all of society.

In the Sumerian myth of Inanna, she is introduced as the Queen of Heaven, ruling with solar focus and vitality. Her sister, Ereshkigal, lives as Queen of the Underworld. Ereshkigal chose to follow her husband when he was banished to the underworld to atone for his abuse of strength and power. Ereshkigal abdicated her own solar authority in subservience to her husband when she followed him to the darkness.

During her rule, Inanna hears that Ereshkigal's husband has died and goes to witness his funeral rites. Inanna begins the descent into the darkness, traveling through seven gates. At each gate Inanna is required to remove an external identifying piece—her jewels, her royal robes, her crown—until, passing through the final door, she stands before her sister, bowed low, naked and exposed. Inanna has nothing but her openness and vulnerability to bring to her sister. Ereshkigal becomes enviously furious that Inanna does not cower, but instead moves to greet her. Inanna, stripped of her external props, is not intimidated. She recognizes that innate power and beauty comes from within, not from a show of strength. Ereshkigal kills Inanna because of this knowledge. Inanna's sacrifice and death mirror the changes we must make individually to grow emotionally and psychologically.

Inanna was not naïve in preparing for her descent. She knew that a price is usually extracted when preparing for journey into the unknown. Inanna gives instructions to her faithful handmaiden should she not return in three days. The handmaiden obtains help, and Inanna is eventually restored to life. She leaves the Underworld with the lunar gifts of open-heartedness and compassion, and a new title. She is now the Queen of Heaven and Earth. Her journey and initiation into the unconscious allow her to become a whole, authentic woman. She is now able to rule with the solar attributes of focused power, passion and energy coupled with the lunar attributes of emotional integrity, vulnerability, and compassion.

In giving up all of her authentic solar power to blindly follow her husband, Ereshkigal must find other ways to show she can garner power, hence her murder of Inanna. The space required to receive the lunar gifts would not have been there had Inanna held on to her solar power. She was able to balance giving up her solar trappings—the jewels, the royal robe—yet still keep her authentic strength as she moved through each gate to meet her sister. Inanna does not become a sentimental woman ruled by emotion upon her return to earth now that she embodies lunar qualities however. She is able to make distinctions between those who show respect and those who do not, and sees relationships in their totality instead of through only one lens.

Now that I understood the solar and lunar aspects of life I was able to look backwards from a different perspective.

Family Life Through a Different Lens

Both my mother and father suffered from the narrow ways society defines gender. My mother played the lunar role exclusively, caring for us children as well as the household, just as my father, dominated by his solar side, was solely responsible for our family's economic needs.

The limitation of these traditional roles became obvious when our economic security was threatened by a diminishing demand for my father's work as a furrier. At that time, it was unthinkable, in the conventional family paradigm, that my mother work outside the house. With chronic economic insecurity taking hold, my father escalated into becoming more of a verbal tyrant, while my warm and gentle mother became more anxious and depressed. She was unable to break out of her role as the "good" wife and mother. Her economic dependence on my father underscored her dependent personality and conventional family roles.

Years later, after I had gained an understanding of lunar and solar influence, these difficulties caused me to view my family's life through a new lens. It became clear that just as my father did not have access to his lunar side, my mother lacked access to her solar power. My parents lived according to the patriarchal myth that made the solar exclusive to men and the lunar to women. It may be more appropriate in certain phases of a relationship for a man to express more of the solar side of consciousness or a woman more of the lunar, but my father's inability to develop emotional sensitivity, and my mother's inability to sense her own power resulted in many tragedies.

What might have happened if my father had been able to admit his fear and vulnerability? Would he have had more patience when we did not accomplish the goals he set out for us? How would our family have been different if my mother had shared the economic burden? Would she have felt more or less entitled? I'll never know, but the lack of options was certainly part of my mother's feeling of helplessness. It's no wonder that my strong identification with my mother, confusing the lunar with weakness, and my struggle to find a way out of my depression, required me to rediscover and reunite both aspects of my "self," the solar and lunar.

Another tragic cost of this skewed traditional upbringing was the suicide of my brother Eugene, about ten years after my mother's suicide.

Eugene was eighteen months younger than I. Almost every night when we were children at the dinner table, he sat silent, watching the screaming battles between my father and me as I reacted to my father's verbal aggressive dominance. At the time, it seemed like Eugene wisely stayed detached and did not confront a no-win situation. However, the cost of his detachment eventually led to a painfully alienated life. Throughout his 42 years, he avoided engaging with others. Eugene never really found his voice.

How would it have been different for Eugene if he had found and come to cherish the solar part of himself and found his voice? When I rescued my own lunar side from Western culture's graveyard, an intrinsic gnawing hunger at last knew satisfaction. Over time I learned to trust my intuition, my feelings, and my judgment, and came to see them as crucial resources.

By using the lunar mode of consciousness as a source of light in the darkness, and by applying my solar abilities to actualize my desires, my life has grown more and more creative. Living in balance is an unfolding adventure that springs from the deepest part of my being. I have integrated this lunar-solar understanding into my practice as a therapist, and developed *Solar Light, Lunar Light*. It is a healing approach which not only solves problems, it brings vitality to the full range of life.

CHAPTER TWO

Healing the Divided Self

*The soul cannot exist without its other side . . . whose nature
can only be grasped symbolically as in . . . the union of the
sun and moon.*

—C.G. Jung

*Great Master Ma was sick. The temple superintendent asked
him, "Teacher, how is your venerable health these days?" The
Great Master said, "Sun Face Buddha; Moon Face Buddha."*

Blue Cliff Record
—Zen koans compiled from 1063 to 1135

Restoring the Solar / Lunar Balance

It is generally agreed that Homo sapiens arose as a distinct entity
about 200,000 years ago. Part of our success as a species is the advan-
tage garnered in having a two-hemisphered brain connected by the
corpus callosum, which allows the flow of information from one side
to the other. It makes sense, from a survival perspective, that nature
would increase the brain's capacity to experience the world by using
two complementary approaches and strategies to process its sensory
data. Our two hemispheres of the brain are like mirror patterns seen
in the unique differences of the function of the sun and moon.

Like the moon, appearing in a different location and size almost
every night, the lunar mind is about processing novelty information.
In this orientation of a spontaneous universe, no time exists except in
the moment—*now* is the only reality. Everything is processed holisti-
cally as a constantly changing collage. Information is carefree, intuitively processed, without rules and regulations. Just as the moon has

regular yet different cycles, lunar cyclical consciousness returns over and over to continually influence physical relationships in nature.

In contrast, the sun comes and goes in a timely sequence every day. This is reflected in the solar brain orientation of pattern recognition, taking moment-by-moment information, which is strung together sequentially. Comparing details from this moment to the next, the solar brain gives us the concept of time; past, present, and future. While lunar consciousness thrives with a holistic image, solar consciousness thrives on details. This is the perfect stage for the development of language, since the solar brain follows rules and regulations for defining and categorizing. As details with language and time emerge, eventually a distinction of "I" occurs, beginning the home of individuality and separateness.

Solar identity—using language—differs from a lunar identity based more on emotions and images. Relationally and intuitively oriented, the lunar brain is more focused on the wholeness of things, the tribe, the earth, and how it all works together and can be expressed in a manner of inclusivity and emotion. Neurological circuits that run autonomously are established in response to these two differently patterned solar and lunar systems. With the brain constantly changing, called "neuroplasticity," we experience the world seamlessly with the solar left hemisphere and lunar right hemisphere operating as two complementary halves rather than as two individual brains. (This seamlessness can be disrupted and is often described by neurologists after events such as stroke, traumatic brain injuries, and some epileptic seizures, for example.)

Of course, men and women are different sexual beings. The differences between male and female brain function is a heated, often emotional, topic. A significant amount of interest and studies have been, and continue to be conducted on behavioral, emotional and intellectual differences between men and women, with many contradictory "scientific" opinions being claimed. If there is a biologically based gender "standard" however, it does not account for individual differences of many women being more dominant, aggressive and logical or many men being more emotionally expressive with strong relational and communication skills. There's still a missing piece in these areas of study. The invitation of seeing both men and women as having a solar and lunar side helps make those murky connections clear. Viewed from a solar and lunar perspective, there is room for a totality of expression in each gender, with all of the possibility formerly characterized as gender-specific to be embodied and expressed by all individuals, regardless of previous labels. By looking at the solar and lunar brains as informing gender, not predetermining it, liberation from the gender stamping of historical and cultural identity offers fresh possibilities for our awakening.

When clients come to me for help with their problems, I search for evidence of an imbalance between their solar and lunar sides. Over time I realized the importance of a complementary balance. Using solar and lunar consciousness allows new solutions to a diverse range of problems to become available.

The soul seeks both sides of its nature. If someone has failed to develop either their solar or lunar aspect, the imbalance usually becomes evident in some form of suffering. Restoring solar/lunar balance enables healing. A good way to describe this process is by telling the stories of men and women I have helped reestablish this balance.

The Solar Feminine

Disguised Solar Power: Anna's Vampire

Dreams belong to the lunar aspects of consciousness. Accordingly, they speak to us in a strange and sometimes improbable language. When clients bring dream images into therapy they often say, "I had a crazy dream last night."

The rational mind does not immediately understand dream images. Yet when it attempts to understand the meaning of a dream, some aspect of the self that had been sleeping awakens. Because the process of interpreting dreams requires the active presence of both sides of consciousness in a complementary way, the discussion of dreams in therapy almost always has a special vitality, and the energy in the room usually grows more intense.

This happened when Anna, a twenty-one-year old college student home for Christmas break, came to see me. She was having a series of disturbing nightmares and hoped I would be able to help her understand them. She began by telling me that she was on probation at school. This was a devastating blow to her already fragile ego. Anna felt lost and confused, not knowing who she was or what she wanted. Her anxiety was so overwhelming that she had not slept adequately for weeks. One night she fell into an exhausted sleep, but was awakened a few hours later from a nightmare that terrified her.

Anna was visibly frightened as she related the long dream. In it, she felt she had to buy a dozen red roses. To accomplish what seemed to be a very important task, Anna found herself entering a flower shop that was owned by a very muscular female with red hair. While she was at the cash register an attractive woman about the same age as Anna came into the store. The woman came over to where Anna was standing, grabbed her, and bit into her neck. She had turned into a vampire and began sucking Anna's blood. That was when Anna woke up screaming. As she finished telling her story, Anna's face was white with terror.

The dream was the key to her dilemma. Anna's vampire represented something she was repressing in herself. If one of the sides of the psyche is not developed, it will often appear in dreams as a menacing figure. Even though dreams belong to lunar consciousness, if the solar side of the mind is repressed, it will emerge in dreams. As Anna and I talked, it became clear to me that the color red—of blood, the roses, and the muscular woman's hair in her dream—represented her need to access her solar feminine side. The bloodthirsty vampire was the starving solar side of herself that had little expression in her life, and hence the vampire was sucking the life force out of her. If Anna could reclaim this part of herself she would be able to use this energy creatively.

I began to tell Anna about the solar and lunar modes of consciousness. Giving some of the history of these symbols to my clients helps them to see that their wounds are not only personal, they are part of a repressed cultural collective unconsciousness. While solar one-sidedness causes a considerable amount of human struggle, it is not from solar energy itself that our society suffers, it is *the lack of balance* that causes problems.

The sun is an archetypal metaphor that lives in both men and women. Even as far back as the Paleolithic era, when hunters associated their spears with the rays of the sun, sunlight was a symbol of power. It is this solar influence that gives us the resources for everything we do, from getting out of bed in the morning and going to work, to pushing past our boundaries into undeveloped areas of our psyches.

As necessary as the solar mode of consciousness is to survival, historically, women have not felt they have the right to develop it. Even today, in Western societies, the solar feminine does not fit the accepted idea of the contemporary woman. Since modern Western culture has repressed the solar feminine, it may seem surprising that in nearly all cultures preceding ours, the solar feminine was highly valued. This aspect of feminine nature was represented by goddess figures who were worshiped for their fiery, fierce, and independent qualities.

The Egyptian goddess Isis, for instance, was a solar goddess in one of her manifestations, as was Aphrodite in Greece. In Japan, the great heaven-illuminating deity Amaterasu, was one such goddess. In Germany a similar figure was called Sunna; in Ireland, she was known as Greine.

Figures such as these help us to reclaim the potential that has been lost. Solar figures appear in many different guises. Anna's muscular red-haired woman was one; and they may manifest as animals, the lioness being one of the more prevalent. But the presence of solar consciousness may not always be so obvious, manifesting in small details, such as the color of a dress or flower.

Anna was fascinated by my overview of solar and lunar mythology. She told me that the main problem in her life was a desire to end a long relationship, one she had wanted to leave for some time, but had felt unable to do. She knew that ending it was an important step toward finding herself. It is the solar mode of consciousness that provides the courage and power for us to put boundaries on different circumstances in life.

Anna's father died when she was eight. Her feelings of loss and subsequent longing for him made it difficult for her to leave relationships with men. She often suppressed her opinions and desires and became whoever men wanted her to be. Anna was afraid that she would be abandoned if she asserted herself. I encouraged her to learn more about the strong aspect of herself emerging in the dreams.

Solar visions have a life of their own. When one is conscious of this fundamental energy, its considerable force becomes available. During our work together, Anna began to confront the challenges in her life. As she developed access to her solar side, she used her studies as a kind of playing field where she could test her strength. By the time she had matured enough to be able to imagine herself as a sun-goddess, she started doing better in school. The next hurdle was to develop her "muscularity." In situations where previously she had felt weak and intimidated, she employed and delighted in using the image of a "muscular woman."

Anna's solar feminine side seemed more and more natural as it emerged. She ended her unsatisfactory relationship. Despite feeling lonely, she was getting to know herself, and that felt far better than being indecisive. She made a commitment to stay in touch with the "muscular" side of herself, and kept at least three red roses in a vase as a daily reminder of her strength. Whenever she acted with courage, her reward was an additional red rose. Symbolic of her strength, her goal was to collect roses.

The psyche naturally seeks balance. As Anna's solar aspect became stronger she dreamed about "the sun rising over a beautiful landscape." A dream voice told her to get "just the right amount of sun," to avoid sunburn. Her unconscious mind was helping to keep the solar and lunar aspects of her "self" in balance. The solar and lunar sides, which are intrinsically neither good nor bad, neither male nor female, are complementary. The solar aspect is never fully effective without its connection to the lunar, and the lunar is more effective with the solar. Each aspect needs the other to keep evolving. The two aspects of consciousness are like a seesaw: both sides are necessary, and the balance between them must be continually adjusted.

As Anna began to live with an integrated consciousness, she discovered a repressed artistic side. Empowered by improved self-esteem, she applied to an art program in a prestigious graduate school, and knew she had come into her own the day the acceptance letter arrived in the mail.

The Solar Masculine

Squashed Inner Fire

In Western culture, our image of masculinity is comprised almost exclusively of solar qualities. But for many men, the strength they exhibit is only a façade. Paradoxically, our culture's rigid definition of masculinity has actually put men out of touch with their authentic solar powers. Rather than acting from authentic solar assertiveness and strength, they behave dogmatically and sometimes aggressively, to compensate for a sense of inadequacy and powerlessness. As a result, many personal difficulties arise from having an underdeveloped relationship with the solar aspects of their "selves."

Tom

In my first meeting with Tom, he told me that he had become severely depressed over a number of years. He was deeply in love and happy with his wife but, for some unknown reason, had lost his sexual desire after the first six months of marriage. Now, two years later, the adventuresome spirit that had highlighted other aspects of his life had also disappeared. Indeed, his nickname was "Fire Ball," and he had always been the one to spark activities among his friends. Tom was losing his "fire" in his professional life, too. He still performed well in his job, but the passion he used to feel for it was no longer there.

Tom's wife was a powerful and successful woman. He was terrified that she would leave him if he did not solve his libidinal problem, and worried that she would mistake his lack of sexual desire as personal rejection. He felt heartsick at the thought of causing her pain. To complicate matters further, his wife was pregnant. He told me that he had mixed feelings about the pregnancy. Initially he'd felt joy, but soon a flood of terror overcame him. The thought of having a child made him even more worried that his marriage could fail. He knew that he could hide from his feelings of sexual inadequacy by distracting Barbara with family matters, but was also aware that his issues were not resolved. Barbara would eventually leave him if he did not seek help. This fear drove him into psychotherapy.

As we talked, I tried to discover what might have shut Tom down. Tom shared stories about his father with me, since he had died recently. His father had been a Marine drill sergeant who ran his family like a platoon. When Tom was young he tried to be a "good" son, rebelling only after he left home. He then experienced a delayed adolescence during which, for the first time in his life, he claimed his authentic solar energy. Now, the responsibilities of marriage and upcoming fatherhood made him feel he had to tow the line again. The only model of male responsibility in a relationship had come from his father. The solar energy and passion, the fire that previously ignited Tom's life, was going out.

It was obvious to me that Tom's relationship with his father diminished Tom's solar energy. In pursuing this question more deeply, Tom told me that his father had been a Korean War hero and a professional athlete. This man expected perfection from his son all the time. If Tom did not get straight A's or excel at sports, his father was disappointed. Tom idealized his father and did everything in his power to be like him. Because he had internalized his father's voice, he would be self-critical when he was not behaving according to the exacting standards his father had set. Although he knew this was irrational, he could not stop blaming himself for being less than perfect. His father had made it virtually impossible for Tom to explore options beyond the "good boy" stereotype.

The issues that Tom faced trying to fit the image of masculinity created the kind of anxiety and insecurity that many men feel, but rarely acknowledge. It is painful and humiliating to feel the disparity between the ideals of masculinity that one is supposed to "be" and their actual experience. Yet in this gap, authentic masculinity can be born.

Tom's story contained one other element worth noting. Because he had experienced a loss of sexual desire, I asked him about his sexuality during adolescence. He told me he had a little world of his own. He would go to the basement to explore his sexual feelings. He was so embarrassed about having any sexual interest that he did not want his mother and sister to know he was talking to a girl on the phone. He stole pornographic material and made random dirty phone calls to neighbors. Tom said that he now called 900 numbers and rented pornographic movies when he traveled. Since he and his wife rarely had erotic encounters, this was his main sexual outlet.

Growing up, Tom was made to feel guilty for his sexual feelings. Pornography often appeals to men who have been told that sexuality is bad when they were young. Sex is portrayed as a "dirty" activity.

Like many men, Tom received contradictory demands regarding manhood as a child. On one hand, he was supposed to repress his sexual energy since it was "dirty." On the other, he got the message that he should be virile.

Tom's challenge was to surrender the ideas he had been taught about manhood and to assume a "beginner's mind." He would then be able to reclaim his authentic solar fire. To achieve this, he would have to know himself, and consciously experience the psychological and physical feelings he had learned to ignore in his quest to satisfy his father's idea of perfection. In turn, he would need to develop his lunar side. Once aware of his real feelings, Tom learned to accept and articulate them. This made him far more effective in the solar realm. In the past, when he had been out of touch with his feelings, he had to push himself to actualize his goals. But fired by authentic desire, he had greater energy and found it easier to achieve what he wanted. He began to have more energy for his work life, and experienced the full force of the sexual energy he had repressed. All aspects of his masculinity were now able to be fully expressed.

I have described how important it is for men and women alike to develop both solar and lunar consciousness. As Tom's story shows, neither solar nor lunar consciousness alone can grow and thrive when it is not in balance. These two parts of the psyche work together, in a complementary way, and help us to perceive, to learn, and to grow. Together, they help us to enjoy life to the fullest.

The Lunar Masculine

The Strength of the Lunar Power: Chris's Surprise

Much to my surprise, my presentations about the lunar aspect of the soul as the "missing piece" in modern masculinity have been well received by the business organizations for which I consult. Concepts like emotional intelligence and empathy are increasingly making their way into the corporate world. Perhaps because the corporate world is so driven, dominated by solar consciousness, it is severely out of balance. Still, in corporate cultures, the main expectation of executives is to meet financial objectives. They must, as is said in corporate culture, "meet the numbers." After one of my presentations, Chris, a man in his mid-thirties and a Vice-President of Marketing, asked if he could meet with me privately. My talk about twin consciousness made him feel that I would be able to understand his dilemma.

During our initial consultation, he told me that after he graduated from a top Ivy-league school, he married, and his wife was now pregnant with their first child. Although he was very successful in almost everything he did, he had also been significantly depressed for many years. Despite the fact that he was an acknowledged leader and was financially successful, he felt like a fraud. He was haunted by the fear that he would be discovered. Chris exhausted himself by constantly performing to meet his or other's expectations. He was so anxious that when he took time off from work he felt guilty. To make matters worse, he learned just before he came to see me that he suffered from Attention Deficit Disorder. (ADD).

ADD is a nervous and emotional disorder characterized by inattention, hyperactivity and impulsiveness. Although it may be overdiagnosed, it is a very real and debilitating disorder. Chris's ADD seemed like an appropriate diagnosis. It prevented him from being able to pay close attention to details, occasionally resulting in careless mistakes and caused him to have difficulty paying continued, focused attention. Distracted and fidgety, he was constantly on the go.

Because he was ashamed of his ADD, he tried to hide the extent to which it affected him. But Chris had other problems at work that he could not hide. The CEO called him into the office and told him that there had been numerous complaints from Chris's colleagues regarding his impatience and verbal aggression. The CEO put him on notice. Chris knew then that he had to do something about his behavior.

The solar masculine is based on contemporary society's primary goal to win at all costs. Chris was competitive not only with himself but also with his sales team. On the wall behind his desk he kept a chart with the name of each member of his team written on a picture of a racehorse. The success of the team member's sales determined the placement of their horse on the chart.

This approach backfired. Instead of working together, his staff competed against each other. They were distrustful and afraid to share their ideas, and were consequently secretive and uncooperative as a team. Chris was caught in his own solar web. He knew that his strategy was failing but did not know how to implement any other approach.

Chris needed to develop his lunar side. The lunar is more receptive, more spacious, and enables interactions with others. Since Chris was a loner, his first challenge was to see that relatedness was as important as the independence he favored. Lunar consciousness complements solar consciousness, it does not substitute for it. The capacity for independence and the ability to form relationships are complementary. They work together; one strengthens the other.

Another important attribute of lunar consciousness is the ability to listen. Listening gives us greater access to lunar consciousness. Though Chris was charismatic and persuasive, his team felt unheard. He was so attached to his own ideas that rather than consider anyone else's, he would try to persuade everyone he was right. When others spoke he seemed lost in his own thoughts. Even if the only ability he learned was to listen, this alone could turn his team around. It would improve his staff's attitude toward him and the quality of their work. I suggested that for the next several meetings Chris not bring up any of his own ideas, but instead acknowledge those he heard from his staff. Though he thought I was being ridiculous, he was so desperate that he was willing to try anything.

Chris was surprised by the results of this approach. His team began to improve immediately. After several weeks of this listening practice, the next step was for him to learn how to interact with others as peers instead of as opponents. This is easier to do if we regularly alternate between acknowledging the other's point of view and expressing our own. The conscious alternation breaks the solar habit of dominating others, and let them know they are valued. Alternating in a rhythm of listening and talking satisfies both people. As Chris began to practice this technique, his sales team became more creative as a group. Everyone did better at meeting quotas.

At the same time, Chris began to notice some relief in his depression and his ADD symptoms started to wane. As he practiced lunar relatedness, Chris likened his new state of mind to the "zone" he felt when playing a good game of golf. "When I just let myself go and merge with the flow of the game, I am a very good player," he said.

In fact, letting go of an obsessive focus on performance, which paradoxically distracts us from the task at hand, is likely to have biological consequences. Solar dominance is not only ineffective in the long run, it can cause stress and stress-related illnesses. Though no medical studies have been done on the relationship between social environment and ADD, it is interesting to note that the corporate environment, with its frenetic pace, rigid agendas, and lofty goals creates exactly the atmosphere that exacerbates and may even cause ADD.

The potential of lunar modes of consciousness is being less and less ignored in the corporate world. The most common strategy to improve performance, the solar perspective, is by focusing on discipline or harder work. This is at best a temporary solution and frequently has a large emotional cost. Chris's story shows that everyone—both the individual and the group—is better off with lunar relatedness. It provides an example of how corporate culture can change from being aggressive and competitive to being cooperative.

The Lunar Feminine

Finding the Inner Ocean

> . . . there is no one to tell me when the ocean will begin.

> *Diving into the Wreck*, Adrienne Rich

Though women are expected to be lunar within a solar society, it is as possible for a woman to be as out of touch with her lunar aspects as a man is. It is easy for a woman to find herself in competitive work and personal situations, that do not meet her deeper needs.

Kate was a predominately solar woman in her thirties. At a point in her life where she was in between careers, she knew that she had to explore herself more fully if she was to find her true vocation. The oldest of six children, Kate's athletic talent as well as her academic competence made her a role model for her siblings. Often the oldest child, whether male or female, takes on the family's solar projections. Some children identify with these projections, while others rebel against them. In view of Kate's many abilities, it was easy for her to play the part of the leader. As a consequence, however, her lunar qualities went undeveloped. After a number of failed relationships, she realized that her life was out of balance.

As Kate became more comfortable talking with me and recognizing what was going on in herself, she realized that her lunar side had been neglected. She was so used to driving herself to accomplish goals that she rarely listened to her hunches. She took pride in her sharp analytical ability. But to access the lunar in a solar world requires both letting go of goals and a greater tolerance of the unknown. Kate's initial reaction to living with lunar consciousness was fear. She didn't know what to do when she did not know the rules, and was afraid she'd look foolish.

Sometimes when clients are having difficulty with transitions, I introduce a story, a myth or a symbol to help them with their fears. In this case, I told Kate about "The Fool," one of the cards in the Tarot. The Tarot is a deck of cards of unknown origin created at least six centuries ago. The cards are used both for self-understanding and fortune telling. They contain twenty-two archetypal images which can speak to different aspects of our psychological depths. The Tarot card "The Fool" casts foolishness in a new light by making it clear that to be creative, one has to take risks, even at the risk of appearing foolish. The writer Annie Dillard describes dropping over the rim of conscious knowledge to find a greater vision:

> *In the deeps are the violence and terror of which psychology has warned us. But if you ride these monsters down, if you drop with them farther over the world's rim, you find what our sciences cannot locate or name, the sub-strata, the ocean*

*or matrix or ether which bouts the rest, which gives goodness
its power for good, and evil its power for evil, the unified field:
our complex and inexplicable caring for each other, and for
our life together here. This is given. It is not learned.*

Kate decided that she would explore this aspect of herself by writing each morning in her journal. Journal-keeping is a safe way to express the feelings of foolishness that may occur when giving voice to the deep self. Writing in a journal also helps to develop reflective consciousness, a lunar capacity that gives birth to the "elusive other" within us, allowing us to see ourselves more fully. Reflective awareness is crucial to the psyche. As we ponder, consider, deliberate and contemplate, we are able to grow into our whole selves.

Lunar reflection is not the same as solar awareness. While the solar modality allows us to analyze and discern, it cannot always embrace or even perceive all of what exists. Lunar reflection, on the other hand, can uncover aspects of our soul that are not apparent to the analytical eye: the parts of the self that are often hidden from critical scrutiny.

Once Kate began to uncover a new dimension in herself, she faced the challenge of bringing her lunar side to life. First, she found a way to express both her lunar and solar aspects in her work. Practicing sensitivity to others, she soon found that she was becoming a highly sought-after management consultant.

But the most difficult challenge was to let herself be vulnerable in relationships. One way she had protected her vulnerability was to pick men who were not strong enough to be caring. As she developed her lunar side, she learned to let go of solar control, and in the process she was drawn to more supportive men.

After years of meeting men who were not her peers she met Doug, whose developmental depth provided the opportunity for her to live fully. I encouraged Kate to trust her intuition, the heart of lunar consciousness. Waiting and being responsive to her inner life rather than initiating action was a different way of being for her.

She liked getting to know this aspect of herself with Doug. Doug felt that she was the first woman who had the strength and capacity to hear him when he was upset, and also to take care of the pragmatic side of life. These were tasks he had never been able to share with a woman before. Together Kate and Doug formed a new kind of relationship, one that comes into being only when there is intuition, consideration and contemplation. Kate found that her soul was touched in a way that it never had been before.

Women dominated by solar consciousness are often afraid of their lunar sides. Traditionally our society has manipulated lunar traits like compassion and empathy in women to keep them in subsidiary roles. But when the lunar is balanced by the solar, the lunar lends strength, depth, and meaning to all our lives.

CHAPTER THREE

Complementarity and Creativity

Complementarity is the fundamental structuring principle in the conscious constructions of human realities.

The Conscious Universe,
—Menas Kafatos, Robert Nadeau

If you bring forth what is within you, it will save you; if you do not bring forth what is within you, it will destroy you.

— Gospel of St. Thomas

The sun and moon, both so visible from earth, are prominent symbols in all cultures throughout the world. They are the largest bodies we see in the sky, crucial points of orientation since quadripeds became bi-pedal and gazed upward. The rising sun heralds the beginning of each day, as the moon denotes nightfall. So profoundly does this shift between night and day affect our consciousness that the difference between them serves as a metaphor for stark contrast.

Like the sun and the moon, there are many other pairs in nature; hot and cold, wet and dry, sweet and sour, life and death. The simplest working distinction between the living and non-living is that living things are able to copy (or twin) themselves out of the raw material they take in from their environment. Even phenomena that are basic to the universe but invisible to the human eye are organized according to this complementarity. DNA, for example, is based on complementary pairs of chemicals, and most living creatures must be able to perceive opposites in order to survive. A simple amoeba differentiates the things it encounters into two groups: food and non-food.

It will move toward one and not toward the other. Human cells are constantly categorizing everything they encounter: they let in some substances and exclude others as they perceive them as either helpful or destructive.

At its most fundamental, we are made of light. Light itself is paired. The electromagnetic energy at wavelengths visible to our eyes (such as colors from a rainbow) is paired with a much larger range of electromagnetic waves that we cannot see (ultraviolet waves, microwaves, and radio waves for example). Although we don't see them, we are affected by these energies. We even feel them, especially at the frequency given off by the earth—about 7.83 Hz—which is almost identical with the frequency of human alpha brain waves. To live optimally, we must literally be in tune with nature.

Every living creature exists in an environment requiring complementary perceptions. Language inherently reflects nature and consciousness in this embodied way. "Embodied" language emerges along with the primal dawning of consciousness itself. This comes forth as a compelling intention to describe instinctive necessities such as hunger, thirst and air. We thus have a language and an "embodied mind" that uses the sensory motor system as a reference for the external world.

Natural complementary patterns should not be confused with Western culture's way of splitting pairs into conflicting opposites. Understanding the distinction between complementary pairs and complementary opposites is fundamental to using *Solar Light, Lunar Light* as a tool of contemporary evolutionary consciousness. Since we are made of light, understanding this differentiation is fundamental to comprehending who we are and how we fit into this universe.

Light has been thought of as streams of particles since the fifth century. This was the prevailing belief and Sir Isaac Newton's view until, in the late 1600's, Christian Huygens proposed that light acted like a wave instead of a stream of particles. This "either/or" formulation—either particles or waves—was debated until the beginning of the 1900s. Einstein, among others including Heisenberg and Pauli, discovered that light was both a wave *and* a particle, which led eventually to the development of quantum physics. Einstein also observed that light is made up of a stream of energy packets called photons.

Even today, students struggle with the problem of duality, acknowledging the simultaneous existence of photons as both particles and waves.

By the beginning of 1925, most of the major figures in physics accepted that photons had wave and particles qualities, but were at a loss to find a theory explaining this phenomenon. The magnitude of trying to understand the wave-particle dilemma was expressed by Werner Heisenberg to Wolfgang Pauli: "What the words 'wave' or 'particle' mean we know not any more; [we are in a] state of almost complete despair." He recognized that what was at stake was the definition of matter itself.

Because quantum physics was about objects that could not be seen, electrons, photons and atoms, the classic solar viewpoint of understanding the world was no longer a sufficient criterion for defining reality. To express this new viewpoint, Einstein wrote, "There is no logical path to these laws; only intuition, resting on sympathetic understanding of experience, can reach them."

In 1927, Niels Bohr insisted that even though the human mind could not imagine an *electron* and *light* as a wave and particle at the same time, those are the qualities of reality that nature has created. Bohr labeled this paradoxical reality of nature—that light and electrons were both a wave and a particle—complementarity. The concept of complementarity led to the discussion that not only was light a wave and particle, but that matter like air, sand, water, rocks and even ourselves, on an atomic level, are composed of waves and particles.

Complementarity is defined as when two or more attributes of an object, such as a wave and particle, are incapable of being observed simultaneously. Those attributes are said to be complementary to each other. Thus, matter exhibits a wave-particle complementarity because, with the complementarity principle, you cannot define one attribute of reality without acknowledging its complementary attribute. The particle perspective offers one view of reality, the wave perspective another. Instead of positing two separate contradictory worlds, Bohr argued that we can combine them into one complex world. The particle and the wave are separate, but are complementary to each other.

Most significantly, both perceptions are necessary to understand this reality completely.

Bohr was convinced that complementarity was relevant, not only so for physics, but also to psychology and life itself. He wrote that this basic idea ". . . bears a deep-going analogy to the general difficulty in the formation of human ideas, inherent in the distinction between subject and object." For example, the figure-ground studies show that when looking at a white vase against a black background, looked at one way, it is a drawing of a vase; looked at another way, it is two faces. We can see back and forth between the two viewpoints, but we cannot see them both at once.

But, the figure *is* both at once. Similarly, we can think of emotions and thoughts as complementary. At the instant that I am thinking a thought, in the same millisecond I will not be conscious of my emotions, and when I am experiencing my emotions, my thought will be complementary. However, both emotions and thought together make up a more complete picture of reality.

Einstein could never accept Bohr's Principle of Complementarity, that the mind's observations are involved in the creation of seeing matter. Einstein felt that ultimately everything had some material non-perceptual reality. Philosophers call this view scientific realism. Over 75 years later, most scientists accept complementarity as a basic principle of nature. Robert Nadeau, a historian of science, and Menas Kafatos, a physicist, have called complementarity the "logic of nature."

It should not be so surprising that Bohr discovered complementarity—nature's logic—when he was in nature. Exhausted from the search for the grand prize in physics—what is matter?—Bohr went to Norway to ski. As he zoomed down the snowy mountain in the cold, crisp air, the mental block that had been impeding his efforts began to disappear. By the time he returned to Copenhagen two weeks later, he had formulated the concept of complementarity to explain the paradox that quantum physics then faced.

The physical exercise of skiing and the beauty of the mountains reawakened the lunar aspect of his consciousness. Using both sides of his psyche, he was able to find an innovative solution to what had seemed like an unsolvable problem.

Historical Perspective

Understanding light as having a twin complementarity ("both/and"), and understanding the importance of the concept of complementarity to the modern mind, we are offered as broad a worldview as possible. The concept of complementarity is not a modern one, although not called by that name. It has been a recurrent theme and reality for over 3000 years. Almost all cultures were organized around complementary pairs of male and female gods and goddesses. It was only with the advent of the Platonic view in Greek culture and Judeo-Christian monotheism that a shift occurred, usually dismissing one of the twin pairs. This is at the root of the issues in our modern thinking.

With the profound paradigm shift from complementarity to monotheism, the sun, as a principle which had previously been both male and female, became associated with masculinity and good, and the moon, which had previously been both male and female, became associated with femininity and evil. Gender complementarity was culturally lost. This dichotomy created a prejudicial gender hierarchy supporting a system of domination. Binary systems in themselves do not have to be prejudicial. Yet in modern consciousness there are two kinds of binary systems: one is judgmental, based on hierarchal reference, and the other is non-judgmental, based on association, and is complementary. It is this complementary world-view that *Solar Light, Lunar Light* advocates.

However, within our culture we are more familiar with the dualistic kind of binary system. We create hierarchies by dividing humanity into categories: upper class and lower class, white and black, masculine and feminine, material and spiritual, and we place one of the pair above the other, consciously or unconsciously. We have also divided the way we think of our experience in this way and so have become alienated from ourselves. *Men are from Mars*; they think too much and are not as good at being emotional. *Women are from Venus*; they are better at emotions than men but not good analytically. We have become so familiar with this prejudicial way of thinking that it becomes automatic, and we fail to notice how limiting it is. If we call emotional sensitivity "feminine" and think of femininity as bad or inferior, we cut ourselves off from the diversity of our ability to sense, understand and respond to our own and other's emotions.

Observer Effect

Solar Light, Lunar Light encourages the use of complementarity as the perspective for how to observe reality. The principle of complementarity and the choices about what is observed is called "The Observer Effect." The "observer," the individual, is necessary before anything can be manifested in the physical universe. This implies that an observation cannot occur without the pre-existence of some sort of perceiver to do the observing. Modern quantum physics gives us insight into understanding the profound impact that the words and images we choose to describe an event have on us, not only internally, on our body and psyche, but also on the events themselves. The quantum notion is that there is no phenomenon until it is observed. We are therefore the co-creator of our realities. From this perspective, our consciousness and ability to expand our mental framework becomes the key to a creative life. A powerful byproduct of this insight of the observer effect in sculpting our reality is that we no longer need to be victims of others or the past, but can empower ourselves in the moment by our conscious awareness.

Physicist Fred Alan Wolf, in his article dealing with the subjective timing of conscious events, indicates that the observer effect occurs whenever we observe our own response to stimuli within our brains and nervous system—provided that we take into account pairs of events—a starting event, which then acts as cause, and a finishing event, which then acts as its effect. A conscious experience occurs if, and only if, these two events occur. Wolf wrote to me that, "What makes this interesting as far as the solar-lunar hypothesis is concerned, is the fact that the dynamics of the connection taking place between the two events involves a quantum . . . solar phase . . . which then reflects the quantum . . . lunar phase . . . We could then put it simply that . . . every conscious event has both solar and lunar components."

Wolf went on to write in this private correspondence,

> *Taking it that the physical world corresponds with the mental world, from which concepts of the physical world apparently arise, it would appear that any mental concepts must involve both a solar and lunar component, in the sense that lunar enlightenment is a reflection of solar action. For example, the arising of a conscious thought would constitute a solar action, while the arising of a second thought or after thought would constitute a lunar action. However, both actions could be experienced at the same time, as we would choose which aspect of our thought process we would remember or take into account. Thus a solar or lunar choice is available to us for every observable event in our lives. 'Light' has a complementary (both/and) solar-lunar choice that is constantly occurring as part of consciousness.*

Complementary thinking enables us to value both parts of a binary pair. It does not force us to choose between one and the other, but instead gives the ability to see each part as a necessary aspect of the whole. This makes perception far more accurate because a balanced approach is in harmony with our environment. Natural cycles are in themselves complementary: night and day, for example, are necessary for the growth cycle of plants because they need both darkness and light to germinate and grow. The human immune system is also coordinated with alternating cycles of light and dark. The 24-hour periods of circadian rhythms coordinate the ensemble of oscillations of the organism with its environments, and the ultradian (20 to 120 minute cycles) rhythms, which synchronize the events in our tissues and organs. Even human consciousness is not a single fixed entity but a dynamic neuropsychological continuum regulated by two chemical systems. One, the *aminergic*, mediates our waking states; and the other, the *cholinergic*, moderates the sleep and dreaming cycle. As states of consciousness alternate continuously between the extremes of waking and dreaming, these chemical systems work in a dynamic equilibrium.

The ancient philosophy of Taoism embodies complementarity as its central organizing principle. The Tao can be roughly stated as the flow of the universe. It is the force behind the natural order that keeps the universe balanced. It shows the possibility of genderless expression, strength and weakness, darkness and light, receptivity and assertion. Its symbol is the Tai Chi [yin/yang], where a dot of light is contained in the darkness and a dot of darkness is contained in the light. This image stands for the mutual interdependence of all mentally-constructed pairs of opposites. It has become a universal symbol of the forces of nature, which is fitting, as it originated as the elements of fire and water. These solar and lunar descriptions beautifully illustrate the innate awareness of complementarity. In the earliest phases of Taoism, the fire of yang and the water of yin were not gendered, but energetically based orientations. With the transition to a Confucian culture based more on morals and ethics than nature, the yang became gendered as man, and the yin as female. This gender stamping is deeply embedded in the psyche of most modern individuals.

However, fire and water are neither male nor female, just as solar and lunar belong to neither male nor female gender.

Complementarity—the logic of nature—is a primary driving principle of nature. In fact, it could be that a solar and lunar, wave and particle reality is a fundamental creation principle of nature and human life.

Creativity

Hierarchical judgments limit human capacities; complementary thinking enhances them. Many extraordinary innovations have resulted from creative processes that use both solar and lunar modes of consciousness. We usually think of science as strictly cerebral and analytical, and, thus, a solar process. But lunar consciousness is also a part of scientific work. When James Watson discovered the nature of DNA in 1956 he used *twin consciousness*—both the solar and lunar parts of himself. According to Francis Crick, who wrote about that process of discovery, it was not only logical thinking that opened Watson's mind to discover the DNA code—it was also playfulness. Crick writes, "The key to discovery was Jim's determination of the exact nature of two pairs . . . He did this not by logic but by serendipity." The openness to find meaning where it is not expected belongs to lunar consciousness. Crick continues, "Play is often important in research." However he points out that solar consciousness is necessary too. "Chance," he says, "favors the prepared mind."

Watson and Crick are among many scientists who have used lunar consciousness in their work. In 1865 Frederick Kekulé had a dream that revealed to him what countless chemists had been struggling to discover: the molecular structure of a carbon atom. His insight opened the door to what is now the field of organic chemistry. Kekulé was apparently neither a particularly good chemist nor an inspiring teacher. He feel asleep after he had been working on trying to reveal the secret of the carbon atom structure, and had a dream that led him to discover a cornerstone of modern science:

> *I turned in my chair to the fire and dozed. Again the atoms were gamboling before my eyes. This time the smaller group*

kept modestly to the background. My mental eye, rendered more acute by repeated visions of this kind, could not distinguish larger structures of manifold conformation; long rows, sometimes more closely fitted together; all twining and twisting in snakelike motion. But look! What was that? One of the snakes had seized hold of its own tail, and the form whirled mockingly before my eyes. As if by a flash of lightning I awoke . . .

The serpent biting its tail gave Kekulé the clue to a revolutionary proposal: molecules of certain important organic compounds are not open structures, but are closed chains or rings.

Kekulé was not alone in describing his use of imagery to solve scientific problems. Einstein, the foremost genius of the twentieth century, had a special gift for envisioning problems in three dimensions. His active imagination played an indispensable role in his experimental formulations, especially in his theories of special relativity. Although Einstein was a brilliant mathematician and logical thinker, he clearly expressed his preference for symbolic thinking (images, lunar) over logic (words, solar). As Arthur I. Miller writes in *Einstein, Picasso*: "For Einstein, creative thinking occurred in visual imagery, and words 'were sought after laboriously only in a secondary stage.'" It was Einstein's ability to use many different forms of representation that helped him to change the way we think about nature. As Philip Franks described it, "When Einstein had thought through a problem, he always found it necessary to formulate this subject in as many different ways as possible . . . "

Many scientists regularly draw on their lunar side in developing their ideas. Barbara McClintock's relationship with the lunar was crucial to her Nobel Prize work. For much of her life she toiled alone in her field, as her brilliant ideas made little sense to her colleagues. Yet before Watson and Crick's discovery of DNA and the molecular revolution, McClintock had discovered some of the deepest, most intricate secrets of genetic organization. What was it that enabled her to see further and deeper into the mysteries of genetics than her colleagues? For her, analytic thought did not provide an adequate means with which to explore the complexities of living forms. Contrary to the scientific doctrine of objectivity, she believed that good science could not proceed without a deep emotional investment on the part of the scientist. It is the emotional investment that provides the motivating force for the endless hours of intense and grueling labor; a lunar orientation. McClintock stressed the importance of receptiveness. She felt that "you must hear what the material has to say . . . and have the openness to let it come to you. Above all, we must have a feeling for the organism." Without her receptivity and ability to listen, McClintock might well have missed the genetic patterns she so brilliantly interpreted.

Just as we tend to think of scientific study as solar, we think of art as emotional, symbolic, and lunar. Analytic thought also plays an important role in the arts, however, although it is often unacknowledged. For example, teachers and students at Germany's Bauhaus, the most influential school of design in the first half of the twentieth century, experimented with new industrial technologies and materials. Paul Klee, Vasily Kandinsky, Ludwig Meis van der Rohe, and Bauhaus founder Walter Gropius, to name a few, created modern architecture, furniture, and practical household items with the objective of unifying art, craft, and technology. They emerged after World War I, with the abolition of censorship and a resulting upsurge of radical experimentation in all of the arts. It should not be surprising that as solar and lunar archetypes are historically the central organizing symbols in creation mythologies, they would emerge after censorship or repression. The re-emergence of complementarity in cultural movements like the Bauhaus is also mirrored individually.

Dance, practiced since prehistoric times, illustrates both solar and lunar consciousness. Indigenous cultures still use dance to express various aspects of a life walking in balance. Whether honoring animal relatives, teaching hunting rituals, reaffirming relatedness or celebrating events, every dance contains within it the harmony that requires both sun and moon energies. However, as Western culture evolved, dance moved away from its connection to the natural world. The codified gestures of the court of Louis XIV, the Sun King, inspired classical dance. With its five basic body positions articulating geometrical relationships between dancers, classical dance epitomizes solar precision in an art form. Structured movement, such as, ballet and courtly dance in Europe, and, in the Orient, the Kabuki tea ceremony, were some of the limited forms of accepted physical expression in arts.

The one-sidedness of the solar organizing principle led to the lunar dynamic breakthrough seen in modern dance.

At the beginning of the twentieth century there were many dancers who, as the developmental psychologist Howard Gardner writes, "evinced dissatisfaction with the ballet." One of the most important innovators of modern dance was Martha Graham. Graham never embraced movement for its own sake. She related motion to feelings she wished to express. "I have to have a dramatic line even in the most abstract things I've done," she declared. "It has to come from one person's experience. I have never been able to divorce dancing from life." Graham clearly states her desire to avoid intellectual abstraction. She once declared, "I don't want to be understandable, I just want to be felt."

Although her inspiration seems to have come from lunar consciousness, Graham's work provides insight into how the solar intellect is also a driving force in the arts. In the process of her choreography, she returned time and again to the writings of Nietzsche and Schopenhauer to understand the power of the human will. For it is human will, as a creative spark of independence, that can serve the body and its flow in movement, or stop us short in a world of ideas. Graham also consulted Freud and Jung to understand how the unconscious works in roles she invented or re-created, balancing the lunar and solar aspects of her work.

Although she may not have been aware of the solar and lunar metaphors embedded in her reference, Graham did, in fact, use this symbolism to describe her art. Once, when she was asked to characterize her goals as a dancer, she referred to a painting by Vasily Kandinsky that features a splash of red against a field of blue. "I will dance like that." This comment reveals another layer of meaning when one understands that in complementarity and creativity, blue is lunar and red is solar. What a perfect way to see the solar spirit: a splash of energy that activates the body toward new dimensions of creative expression, while the lunar holds this solar event in a sea of intuition and feeling.

Ignoring solar consciousness in other art forms can be as detrimental as ignoring the inspiring lunar. According to writer Susan Griffin, "Inexperienced writers often shy away from editing and rewriting."

In other words, they overvalue their lunar and undervalue their solar skills. "Paradoxically," she says, "they often end up discouraged when they never quite finish their work or are not happy with what they have written. Some solar work polishes the gem and makes its beauty visible."

The lunar capacity to innovate requires solar energy. Bringing new material into cultural awareness calls for a significant amount of solar courage. The reverse is also true: solar energy is fed by lunar insight. But in our solar society, history often remembers the solar dimensions of achievement and forgets the lunar contribution.

Complementarity Within Ourselves

Complementarity describes the nature of consciousness as well as reality. Just as an electron can appear as a particle and as a wave, reality can appear entirely differently depending on whether it is viewed through a lunar or a solar lens. For instance, in a lover's quarrel, though a man may be certain he loves his partner, she can be equally certain that he is rejecting her.

Different perspectives also exist within one person. In a very short amount of time, perhaps simultaneously, we might describe the weather as dull and gloomy, or soft and poetic. The solar aspect of our psyche may perceive a foggy day as annoying because we had planned to go to the beach, but at the same time we find ourselves admiring the beautiful movement of the fog through the trees and dunes. Our emotional reality sees *both* perspectives.

Our highly linear society has a predisposition toward over-simplification; sound bites in the media, a single cause for a complex problem, a magic-bullet solution, a good or bad person. The fact is that much of the time our feelings are complex and contradictory. Societal leanings have us believe we have to choose between our internal contradictions, that it must be only one and not the other, leaving no room for complexity. This leads to a feeling of being trapped, ambivalent, or indecisive, which can lead to feeling paralyzed and unable to think creatively. When this happens, it helps to remember complementarity. It can be both liberating and empowering. If we can accept the nuances of our feelings and their apparent contradictions, both sides of the inner conflict speak to us. This can lead to an original way of thinking or to an unexpected course of action. When we embrace both sides of our own consciousness, including our inconsistent feelings, we find that we are more capable of loving ourselves. This allows us to be more grounded. The grounding and acceptance of ourselves helps us to become more capable of loving others, and of loving life itself.

Complementarity is crucial to our understanding of the universe, our own consciousness, and creativity. When a problem seems unsolvable, it is likely that either our solar or lunar consciousness is not accessed. A popular misconception of Freud is that he was a cold analyst who sat quietly beside the couch and offered little of himself. Many of Freud's former patients tell us how engaged and expressive he was with them however. The technically oriented (solar) approach, which is now the norm in Freudian therapy, actually began only with the expansion of Freudian analysis in the United States.

Poet Hilda Dolittle, better known as H.D., was analyzed by Freud from 1933 to 1934. She wrote an account of her treatment that became a tribute to their work together. Freud felt that the main task of analysis was to make the unconscious conscious. Rather than being detached and unresponsive, he was fascinated and passionately engaged with her, even to the point of using anger to advance their work. In their first meeting H.D. describes him beating his fist on the headpiece of the couch. While this type of emotional engagement would seem out of place in most contemporary therapy sessions, H.D. was aware of Freud's intentions. "Even as I veered around, facing him, my mind was detached enough to wonder if this was some idea of his for speeding up the analytic content or redirecting the flow of images." Countering the impression that Freud was a silent and stony faced therapist, she said, "Freud had a hundred faces."

H.D.'s description of Freud suggests that the success of his work was very much connected to a complementary awareness derived from the balance of solar and lunar consciousness (although not acknowledged as that.) Departing from the sterile environment of the American mid-twentieth century model of modern psychology, therapy is often improved when therapists learn to use both modes of consciousness in the process of healing. As most therapists who have broken from traditional analytical practices now acknowledge, analytical understanding is far greater in a relationship in which both trust and intimacy have been established.

The nature of consciousness and the nature of the universe mirror each other. Psychologist William James notes that "consciousness may be split into parts which coexist but mutually ignore each other. More remarkably still," he said, "they are complementary."

Both solar and lunar consciousness are needed for creative endeavors of all kinds. Creativity requires us to alternate between both of these modes of consciousness. This is also true for every aspect of life. Whether in personal relationships, family life, or community, complementarity enriches our daily experience and makes us feel whole.

CHAPTER FOUR

Self-Esteem and Expectations

There's no success like failure, and failure's no success at all.

—Bob Dylan

Fear of Failure

We live in a heroic culture. In a society dominated by solar values, we are bombarded by countless images of perfection, ideals we are encouraged to emulate. Consequently, many of us find ourselves working toward goals that are unattainable: a flawless body, an impeccable career, a perfect marriage. Yet within the society that projects these ideas, loss of self-esteem is a major problem. No wonder so many of us are plagued by fear and anxiety around failure. With high expectations, we strive to better ourselves while harboring secret doubts and a gnawing sense of emptiness.

Underneath all these efforts to improve is a sense of inner defeat, disappointment, and loss. As we try to make ourselves into our idealized image, consciously or unconsciously, we reject who we really are. When we openly, or even more often covertly, disparage or hate ourselves, a response of shame is prompted.

Shame has serious consequences. The obsession with body image that many women in particular have or believe that men have about women's bodies, demonstrates a striking example of the power of an image and how it can become deadly. Today, many young women are intent on losing weight to emulate thin models. This obsession, a condition called anorexia, can end up with women starving themselves, and has claimed numerous lives.

Very successful people also risk an obsession with image. Feelings of shame that go hand in hand with the roller coaster of success and failure can be fatal. The first enlisted man to rise to the top job of U.S. Chief of Naval Operations, Admiral Jeremy Michael Boorda, committed suicide in May 1996. Hours before he shot himself, Boorda, 57, appeared "concerned" about queries *Newsweek* magazine had made about the pins of valor he had worn on his Vietnam War ribbons for years. Boorda lied about the accolades he'd legitimately earned versus those he claimed. The driving motive for his successful suicide was the shame of being discovered with a lack of personal integrity. This emotional mortification was far greater than his fear of dying—in combat or by suicide.

Feelings of inadequacy, shame, and perfectionism go hand in hand with a heroic culture. Our solar society has created abstract ideas about who we should be and how we should live. The obsession with perfection in Western culture goes back to the Hellenic age, when the philosopher Plato promulgated his theory of original forms. He believed that truth could not be known through the senses. He proposed instead that there was a world of ideas which could be known only through reason and logic. He placed the highest value on the ideal of beauty, which was, for him, synonymous with good. Not coincidentally, Plato equates beauty and good with the sun, which he sees as masculine—the hierarchy under which Western society continues to labor today.

What is harmful is our habit of rejecting real goodness and beauty in favor of what we think ought to exist. The rejection of who we really are in favor of an abstract ideal occurs when solar values are inflated over lunar values. While solar consciousness employs logic and abstraction, the lunar mind knows through sensual detail, emotional exchange and self-reflection. It is through the lunar aspect of the psyche that we know and experience our real emotions. To attain self-acceptance, the first step toward self-esteem, we must first know ourselves as we really are. Empathy for ourselves and others is based on knowledge and acceptance. In a balanced psyche, self-acceptance is accompanied by the ability to discern and distinguish, to think logically and abstractly, so that self-knowledge can be placed in a larger context. But without the balance of lunar insight, the mind replaces real sensations and feelings with ideals and abstractions of humanity instead of real flesh and blood human beings.

Since most of the cultural ideals are unattainable, their pursuit tends to end in failure and a chronic feeling of disappointment. Meanwhile, overlooking who we really are, we feel a hunger for the vitality of life that comes naturally from self-acceptance. This lack becomes part of a vicious cycle. When we do not accept ourselves, we avoid the introspection that leads to the emotional integration we need to live full lives. We pay a heavy toll for our perfectionist ideals. Some women pursue expensive and painful surgical procedures to look younger. Some men are never satisfied with their accomplishments and literally work themselves to death.

Western culture is driven by heroic expectations that lead to two of the major psychological problems that plague our society today, low self-esteem and narcissism. Narcissists do not love themselves as much as it appears. They have a fragile, superficial and ultimately false image of who they think they ought to be. The term "narcissism" was taken from a Greek myth. Narcissus was a handsome young hunter who continually rejected the countless suitors who fell in love with him. One day, as he bent over a pool for a drink of water, he saw himself and fell in love with his own reflected image. This attraction became a consuming passion which destroyed him. Narcissus died obsessed with his own image. Though low self esteem and narcissism may appear to be opposites, they are in fact two sides to the same coin. Both syndromes are caused by a lack of self-love.

Freedom from Low Self-Esteem and Dependency

Those who suffer from low self-esteem are as dependent on the opinions of others as narcissists. For centuries, traditional Western society raised women to serve and please men. The myth of Narcissus portrays one such woman, the nymph, Echo who fell passionately in love with Narcissus. The goddess Hera was served by Echo. Echo betrays Hera by detaining her with talk, allowing Hera's husband Zeus to escape undetected in his trysts. Hera curses Echo, causing her to remain silent until someone else speaks to her; she then can only repeat the last words of the speaker. Echo thus becomes the perfect foil for Narcissus. By echoing, repeating back everything Narcissus says, she mirrors back to him his idealistic imaginings. They participate in a superficial give-and-take, losing any sense of who they are and what they really feel.

Women who echo men instead of speaking for themselves are out of touch with their authentic feelings. They lack empathy for themselves and perhaps for others too. Neither compliance, nor the desire to please, are the same as empathy.

Another route to the recovery of an authentic emotional life is through the physical sensations we have in our bodies. Because the body and the mind are not separate, physical feelings can often reveal our hidden or unconscious emotions.

Marilyn

Marilyn came to me during an unhappy period in her life. She was highly critical of herself, especially of the way she looked. She felt she was overweight and every attempt she made to diet failed.

Many women who are so intensely focused on their bodies are unaware of what they are actually physically feeling. They are not really paying attention to their bodies, but to a cultural fantasy image that idealizes young, thin figures. No wonder then that so many cannot lose weight; we can repress hunger only so long before it comes back with a vengeance. This creates a vicious circle of failure: the loss of self-esteem increases, which leads to more hunger, which leads to more eating. A good way to develop self-knowledge, especially for people who are obsessively focused on body image, is to learn to tune into their real physical emotions instead of echoing society's opinions.

Marilyn was afraid to consider what her body wanted because she feared she might be overwhelmed with hunger. But bodily hunger can also be misread; sometimes what the body really longs for is food for the soul. As she learned to pay close attention to what she was feeling, Marilyn became aware of her body's desire for more activity.

This insight alone did not assuage her hunger. She added long walks to her week and took up tennis. Although she enjoyed these activities, she remained unsatisfied in a way she could not define. I encouraged her to explore memories relating to the longings she still felt. I suggested she try "free association," a technique used in therapy, which requires that we give up any assumptions about our history. It allows our mind to wander until we experience an emotional charge. We then take an emotion or dream image that emerges as a form of intuition, a lunar activity that enables us to enter a fertile void of another kind.

When Marilyn explored what associations she had with movement, she felt sadness. She remembered a junior high school dance class during which the teacher, in front of Marilyn's friends, shamed her for her clumsiness. While she was telling me this she broke out in tears. In a muffled tone, she said she had been humiliated in public about her physical awkwardness many times. She realized that this was why she began to overeat.

After some resistance, Marilyn signed up for a class in ballroom dancing. Although she felt nervous anticipating the first night, she was surprised to find a group of warm and friendly people of all ages and sizes. They welcomed her into the group. As the evening went on, Marilyn experienced her body in ways she hadn't since childhood. She loved what she was beginning to feel, both emotionally and physically. She signed up for more classes.

Behind Marilyn's unrealized wish to dance were profound feelings of disappointment. She was in the habit of thinking of herself as someone who could not do things, rather than as someone who could. Now, she began to reclaim her power. One of the ways she became so out of touch with the "I can" attitude was through overeating. It both repressed strong surges of energy and made her feel like a failure at dieting. She blamed her body for her constant feelings of hunger. In dance, her body became a source of healing, and she returned to her authentic feelings and real sense of power.

Discovering Empathy: Jayson's Story

Over many months I worked with a young man who suffered from a narcissistic wound. He came to me because he was lonely and unable to commit to anyone. Like Narcissus, he had gone from lover to lover, ending relationships as soon as he found some small flaw in it.

When he was a child Jayson's parents admired him, but he never felt really loved. An unusually beautiful boy, his parents also constantly bragged about him, claiming a range of academic talents that he did not possess. He now transferred these impossible standards to each of his potential mates.

Empathy, a lunar capacity, is crucial to everything we do in life, but is especially important in relationships. Jayson had not developed his lunar side, and empathy, in particular. He had never really received empathy in his childhood. Though his parents showered him with praise, he felt it was for a puppet son they had invented. Even as their praise made Jayson feel like a sham, he was afraid that he would disappoint them. Admiration and praise are poor substitutes for empathy. To be able to empathize with another, we need first to be able to empathize with ourselves.

The Fertile Void: A Rich Field of Possibility

Healing requires change. Change requires that we relinquish habits, patterns and ideas about ourselves that are familiar, safe and comfortable, though they may be harmful. Though idealizations and false selves lead to feelings of emptiness, giving up what we are used to results in a sense of loss. It takes courage to enter what feels like a void. But with time and perseverance, this void becomes a rich field of possibility as authentic feelings arise.

Since the first step in the development of self-empathy is self-knowledge, Jayson had to begin to tell the truth about himself and express his real feelings. His first attempts were tentative, but as I listened to what he said with acceptance and empathy, he experienced the all-important mirroring we all need to feel whole.

Jayson was then able to begin to develop empathy for others, and experienced a dramatic breakthrough on a hunting trip he had taken with a group of other men. Jayson's prowess as a hunter had become a major part of the identity he had constructed. He was known as a very good marksman, but now he found himself missing his prey almost every time he took aim.

With questioning, Jayson realized that the reason he had been pulling the trigger a few seconds too late was that he had stopped to look at the animal he had in his sight. On his next trip he realized that he felt ambivalence toward shooting these creatures. He had begun to feel empathy for them.

I encouraged Jayson to enter the "fertile void" on his next trip by going out into the forest without attempting to shoot any prey. The "fertile void" is a synonym for the Zero Point Field in quantum physics. Paradoxically, this vacuum is filled with energy. The electromagnetic zero-point field is loosely considered as a sea of background electromagnetic energy that fills the vacuum of space. In Buddhism the fertile void is called "emptiness." I suggested he observe the animals he saw and note his own feelings. This was to be a turning point in his life. Moved and fascina ed by the wildlife around him, he found that the animals and forest alike seemed to draw forth his own deepest authenticity. He began to sketch the animals he observed. He feared the ridicule of his fellow hunters, but when he showed them his drawings they were impressed and encouraged him to continue. Though glad for their friendship, more significant to him was the fact that he did not feel as dependent on their praise. He had discovered who he was and what he genuinely wanted.

Relationships require us to mirror and witness those we love with an open heart. Narcissists seek admiration, not intimacy. They see those around them as an audience for giving them praise. As Jayson's self-knowledge grew, his need for admiration relaxed. He found himself listening to others. For the first time he began to experience real intimacy, first with friends and acquaintances and finally with a lover. He recognized that in order to experience this, he had to let go of the false persona and mask he had created that prevented him from authentic exchange.

The Loss of Integrity: Bill's Depression and Recovery

The fertile void, a place of silence and suspended judgment in consciousness, is also the state of mind which is necessary for creativity. This is so whether in the arts or in creating a life. Those who continually live in a fertile void—the zero point field of unlimited energy potential—and live with integrity, gain access to their own creativity. Conversely, many psychological symptoms such as depression and anxiety occur when this integrity is lost. This loss is often preceded by the effort to measure up to performance standards imposed by society.

Since childhood, Bill had been obsessed with becoming a doctor. Though this desire was genuine, it was fueled by perfectionist ideals. He thought that he should be a perfect doctor, and he had very rigid ideas about how to become one.

Bill knew that the competition to get into medical school was brutal. Although he was on the dean's honor roll in college, he felt insecure about his innate intelligence. He attributed his great academic success to obsessive studying at the expense of a social life and other interests, particularly music.

Bill was aware that his habit of hard work had a shadow side, but he got into medical school. While there, in his late twenties, he was diagnosed with cancer. When his cancer went into remission, he carefully controlled the stress in his life.

Bill did become a doctor. Twenty-five years later, he was physically well and had a successful medical practice but was, nonetheless depressed. Though in many ways his life seemed perfect, he told me that he found it empty.

Perfectionism and the lack of an inner life become a self-perpetuating cycle. Those who have lost touch with themselves seek to fill the void with successful accomplishments. Often, they become so over-worked and stressed by reaching one goal after another that they never take the time to know their own inner desires. Even when stress and overwork are eliminated, their single-minded focus on success can lead to feelings of emptiness. This is because the ideas most people have of success are defined externally by authority figures or society.

Solar culture is replete with expectations. Some of these expectations, such as getting good grades or finding a lucrative profession, are communicated directly. Others are communicated more subtly, through advertisements or competitive games. Participation in corporate and government work frequently requires competitive behavior. Since most of us never question these expectations, we find ourselves leading uninspired lives, driven by drab routines.

I have had many patients like Bill in my practice, men who have internalized the expectations of a solar society. When a man is governed by these standards, he moves further and further away from his internal life, rejecting who he is and his authentic desires in the process. His subsequent buried feelings of loss and dissatisfaction compel him to repeat this cycle compulsively.

To develop an internal life, each of us must be willing to become unattached to the idealizations we have internalized and rediscover our real desires and feelings. To live with integrity, Bill would have to find what desires were buried inside his fear of imperfection. By listening to our intuition we can discover these deeper aspects of ourselves—the parts of our soul yearning to become manifest. But, our solar culture neither values nor encourages the development of intuition, and sometimes teaches us to fear it.

As Bill began to listen to his intuition, he waited for his unconscious to suggest a path that would help him live more authentically. The first ideas that came to him were studying acupuncture and returning to playing the cello. The thought of pursuing what they wanted gave him a feeling of deep inner joy, yet he was also frightened. He feared that his efforts might create stress and a recurrence of cancer.

Bill's anxiety about his own perfectionism was realistic. In a solar society, to relinquish an expectation and follow one's intuition triggers the fear of a loss of identity, which activates the fear of death. Underneath the solar goal of domination is the unconscious belief that our idealizations keep us safe, protect us from death, or from "going crazy." Ultimately nothing can protect us from death, but our idealizations and expectations can keep us from being fully alive.

I suggested to Bill that there are different, lunar ways of approach that would not trigger his perfectionism. I often introduce my clients to *active imagination* to help them gain new learning patterns. The technique of visualization is commonly employed by therapists to treat a variety of issues, ranging from anxiety to lack of self-confidence. Imaginary experiences can help us learn in a natural, playful way, as children do before they are taught that "learning is work." Through images, we are able to access untapped resources within that mirror whatever it is we seek to learn.

Yo-Yo Ma was Bill's favorite cello player. I suggested that he imagine Ma as his teacher, and to be open to new sensations as he gave his imagination permission to listen and learn in a different way. I asked Bill to listen to his favorite recording of Yo-Yo Ma before our next meeting with this new intent. Bill was asked to sit in his favorite chair with his eyes closed and to feel the vibrations of the music in his body. The next time we met, I asked him to recreate this experience in his mind's eye as we tried an experiment. I told him that he would hear a knock on the door and if he opened it, he would discover Yo-Yo Ma there, ready to give him a cello lesson. If Bill were to let Yo-Yo Ma sit down next to him and start playing in his imagination, he could learn from the master he admired.

To deepen his sensory experience, I asked Bill to feel the cello between his legs, the bow in his hand, and the subtle vibrations inside him of the music being played. With a little practice in active imagination Bill reported that he was learning with greater ease.

Several experiments have shown that active imagination can affect athletic and other performances positively. Though this new pedagogy was in sharp contrast to his previous training, these studies appealed to Bill's solar side and gave him the confidence to follow them.

Bill continued to use his intuition while he studied acupuncture. Although acupuncture is an alternative form of medicine in the West, it is taught in some medical schools, utilizing the same solar approach as Western medicine. To prepare for his studies, I encouraged Bill to experience the acupuncture points in his own body. He became the patient of an acupuncture master. Bill rarely paid attention to his body and this experience was in sharp contrast to his earlier education, in which the mind dominated. Learning had been a great passion in his younger years. If he paid attention to his physical feelings, he discovered, it was safe for him to continue his studies.

Sensual knowledge not only reveals hidden emotions, it can also provide us with a way to become free of our solar idealizations. In a society that values abstract goals, physical sensations rarely conform to rigid expectations and are often repressed. Paying attention to them again can reverse that repression and break the hold that idealizations have on our minds.

Eventually Bill incorporated this more relaxed way of learning. As children play, they couple their physical awareness with their mental process. This bypasses solar, perfectionistic expectations and they can learn more readily, a process that Bill was re-learning. He regained his ability to enjoy life and, with this freedom to grow and learn without solar pressure, his depression vanished.

The Parts We Play: Mythological Parallels

Among the most common expectations to inhibit emotional growth are culture's definitions of masculinity and femininity. To break free of harmful patterns we need to free ourselves from the straightjacket of gender. For Bill to use his intuition in active imagination, for instance, he had to break through his overwhelming prejudice against the lunar masculine in our culture. For Jayson to become authentic, he had to give up his identity not only as a hunter, but also as a predator in relationships. If we are to develop more authentic lives, we must break the bondage of culture's limited ideals, despite the dominance of the solar fantasies, including descriptions of masculinity and femininity.

Marilyn had to learn to not be subservient to society's idea of denying her hunger and pleasing men. Echo's willingness to betray Hera and protect Zeus mirrors Hera's decline and the start of the shift to a patriarchal orientation. Before she was depicted as Zeus's consort, Hera was a mother sovereign goddess. Zeus was considered the intruder in Hera's matriarchal rule.

One way to understand Echo, and today's society in this patriarchal culture, is that we are forced to abandon our own inner lives to act in service to a masculine ideal. The caution of this betrayal of self exists within the same myth. Hera, the solar goddess, curses Echo. Banished, Echo discovers Narcissus and becomes enamored. He dismisses her. She pines away from her longing for him, leaving just her cursed voice, her echo. Nemesis, a lunar goddess, curses Narcissus for this. Daughter of night, Nemesis is considered one of the most powerful of the divinities by the Greeks, who showed her great respect. Her function was to see that everyone played their role allotted by destiny. Because pride and hubris disturb the natural order of the universe, Nemesis punished pride in all its forms. Narcissus' pride in his own beauty contributed to Echo's death. Hence, Nemesis curses Narcissus to spend the rest of his life admiring his reflection. He too dies, but is transformed into the flower bearing his name.

When Nemesis first arose in the matriarchal-based, mythological time of the Titans, intuition was more valued than abstract thought. Transcending the realm of logic and objectivity, Nemesis came forth from the inner world of emotions as well as from creative imagination. Because she is a lunar goddess, Nemesis has reflective consciousness: she is always true to herself.

Self Reflection

As the myth shows, a narcissistic personality can only see his or her idealized fantasies of reality and misses the opportunity of self-knowledge or authentic knowledge of others. However, the human psyche has both the ability and the need to see itself clearly. The lunar capacity for reflective consciousness is essential to the development of the authentic self, and occurs naturally in children who feel loved. This is another reason why unconditional love for children is so important.

The lack of this love leads to both low self-esteem and narcissism. It creates the fear that we will not be loved if we express our real feelings. Healing requires the expression of real emotion; it leads us to self-knowledge, but to let go of idealizations can be frightening. The solution lies in the nature of the human soul. As much as we want to be loved, we also long for the truth.

It is interesting that the same episode in the myth of Narcissus that signifies self-idolatry also offers a path to the authentic self. In Ovid's *Metamorphoses*, where we find the oldest version of the myth, Narcissus finally realizes that the youth he has fallen in love with is himself. "Alas, I am my self the boy I see," he cries. Despairing over what seems a cruel joke, he commits suicide. But before he dies he says, "My own reflection does not deceive me." This offers the promise of true self-knowledge. Thus this version of the myth has another level of meaning which speaks more to transformation than to mortality. A flower grows on the spot where he dies: the narcissus. If we are to flower, we must relinquish our masks and let the false selves we have created die. In place of what we give up, we gain our own wholeness. To live in integrity means to experience a state of unity between inner ideas, images, emotions and our outer behavior. Ralph Waldo Emerson said, "Nothing is at last sacred but the integrity of your own mind. Absolve you to yourself, and you shall have the suffrage of the world." This is the secret to living well.

The solar tendency to substitute idealized images for reality has wreaked havoc in many lives. It has done so both directly and through the social problems it creates. The chapter that follows examines just one of the problems that comes from the repression of lunar consciousness.

CHAPTER FIVE

Holy War, Lunar Values and Terrorism

Terrorism, like viruses, is everywhere. There is a global perfusion [sic] which accompanies any system of domination as though it were its shadow, ready to activate itself anywhere, like a double agent.

The Spirit of Terrorism and Other Essays
—Jean Baudrillard

Bin Laden and Evil

The two primary modes of thinking that constitute human consciousness are complementary. One is intuitive, sensual and emotional. The other is analytical, focused and goal oriented. Both modes, lunar and solar, work best in tandem. Their internal collaboration creates balance in thought, perception and emotion. In our culture solar consciousness has become so dominant, and lunar consciousness so diminished, we have lost our symmetry. We think without feeling, yet underneath our logic we are driven by unexamined passions.

The destructive habit of mind we have inherited shares a history with the war on terrorism. The events of September 11, 2001 in New York City set in motion the latest phase of an epic conflict, one that began thousands of years ago with the development of three religions: Judaism, Christianity and Islam. All three grew out of cultures that originally worshipped a variety of gods and goddesses. The single solar "jealous" god and the culture from which it sprang necessitated the repression of the other deities and the values they represented.

At first glance this theological history may seem irrelevant to the dilemma we face now. While Osama bin Laden and his followers describe the war on terrorism as a "holy war" against infidels, justifying their acts of violence, we fail to see that we are also conducting a religious war.

We pride ourselves on the separation of church and state, but the truth is considerably more complex. Even in the official language of our government, less than secular motivations can be detected. In remarks made after the bombing of the World Trade Center, President Bush used the words "evil" and "crusade" to describe the terrorist acts and our response to them. Although the Bush Administration made an effort to distinguish between the Islamic religion and terrorism, the use of the word "evil" has continued to work at cross purposes to this policy. It unconsciously expresses religious judgment.

"Evil" has powerful religious connotations. When Bush referred to bin Laden as "the evil one" he was invoking a centuries-old tradition of religious dualism, which divides the world into good and evil, those who serve God and those who serve Satan. It is relevant that Bush is a proclaimed born-again Christian. His language tells us that just as he demonizes our opponents he also identifies the United States with a monotheistic God.

Some organized religions believe that other religions and religious preferences are evil. This tendency is particularly exaggerated in fundamentalist sects. Ideas of good and evil are used to describe an individual person's internal conflict. When we, as individuals, characterize the other as "evil," that "other" is an unconscious aspect of ourselves that we deny. The same occurs between nations. When we fail to accept qualities like evil and aggressiveness as a part of our national identity, we project it onto a nation we view as "other."

Though bin Laden's action was destructive and immoral, the word "evil" to describe him prevents us from acknowledging our own aggressive behavior. The denial that accompanies projection undermines our capacity for self-reflection. We were shocked and horrified by bin Laden's attack on innocent Iraqi civilians, yet within a few weeks we began bombing raids that led to the deaths of thousands of innocent Afghanistan. Instead of acknowledging the ethical consequences of our actions, we described these deaths as "collateral damage."

The religiosity of our rhetoric, which paradoxically allows us to fault another even as we deny our own ethics violations, has other implications too. The monotheistic tradition we share contributes to violence in a multitude of ways. With the assertion that there is only one god comes the belief that there is only one religion, one truth, and one perspective that is valid. Such a belief gives rise to seemingly insolvable conflicts.

Abraham: the Father of Us All

It is generally recognized that individual conflicts are likely to be rooted in relationships with parents, but what is frequently ignored is that a culture's unresolved issues are also likely to have been formed in the culture's early evolution. Understanding this evolution is especially relevant since all three religions claim the same mythological father, Abraham.

The three religions involved in the current Middle East crisis are all competitively monotheistic, yet they also share many sacred texts and stories. Sharing a mythological past could potentially create a bond between these religions (both Judaism and Islam claim the agreement between Abraham and God as the foundation for their religious beliefs), but both religions also claim exclusive possession of a covenant with God. In the Judeo-Christian tradition, Abraham's first son Ishmael, born of the Muslim slave woman Hagar, represents the alienated stranger, often seen as a symbol for heresy. He is the outsider who has no place in the tradition. To the Muslims on the other hand, Isaac, child of the Jewess Sarah, is an oppressive foreigner who must be rejected and repressed, as he usurps legitimate claim and power.

Regardless of competing claims, all three religions share in Abraham a solar-based figure. He represents a set of desires and designs that, in preceding cultures, have been connected to gods and goddesses associated with the sun. They, in turn, were connected with the solar aspect of human consciousness. In those cultures, a range of solar deities can be found whose attributes reflect strength, protectiveness and power, along with the ability to assert control. Correspondingly, they reflect the clarity of mind that comes from analytical thought.

These solar deities were, however, balanced by another group associated with the moon. The group consisted of both gods and goddesses whose attributes reflect the lunar side of consciousness: cooperation, and emotional and sensual awareness.

Remnants of both lunar and solar deities are found in the story of Abraham. Abraham appears at the beginning of the Judaic history and, hence, Christian history as well. According to the Old Testament commanded by Yahweh, Abraham was given a special destiny. He was to become the Father of Israel, and as part of this divine bequest his descendants were to claim the land of Canaan now Israel. But according to the same tale, Abraham is also the father of another people. As the story goes, because Abraham's wife Sarah was not able to bear children, she told him to sleep with her Egyptian maidservant, Hagar, to build a family through her. Thus, through Hagar Abraham fathered the child Ishmael, whom later Judaism generally viewed as wicked. Contrarily, Islamic tradition viewed Ishmael as a prophet.

According to the same myth, claimed as a story of origin by both Judaism and Islam, the Lord appeared to Abraham years later and declared a covenant between Abraham and his descendants. He promised that he would bless Sarah, now ninety, with a son, to be named Isaac. Following Isaac's birth, Sarah, who was jealous of Hagar's son Ishmael, asked Abraham to banish Ishmael, which he does. This solar-lunar, brother-brother conflict is one of the core issues tearing apart the modern world.

As with any myth, this story has more than one level of meaning. It denotes the birth of an intimate connection to one jealous god. The narrative also depicts the cultural and psychological transformations that were necessary to fulfill the aspirations toward empire held by both cultures. To complete this transformation a shift had to occur from the cooperative tribal, lunar consciousness of the old way of life, to the solar individual consciousness that exists within any competitive social order.

Abraham's covenant elevates both individual rights and private property rights above the collective good. No longer do members of the tribe have the imperative to take care of each other. Solar ownership mentality incorporates not only possessiveness of articles and property, but the owning and controlling of the lunar expression of women, and the religious experience of God. Even more crucial to this shift, a single god was claimed as the only god. This solar god distanced the human personality from lunar expression. With the inflation of the solo solar sky god and the repression of the lunar earth spirits, the mind and the intellect dominate instincts and nature. The culmination became a god with human, masculine features placed above all of nature, including the sun and the moon. The descendents of Abraham were alienated from the earth. As heirs of this new cosmology, we no longer see ourselves as part of the whole of nature. Instead, we strive for mastery over nature and over each other.

This way of thinking is deeply ingrained in our shared cultural consciousness. Centuries before the story of Abraham was told, the people of the Middle East, including the Hebrews, worshipped a range of gods and goddesses who represented diverse aspects of nature. Abraham's new god Yahweh evolved from just one god of many in the larger pantheon, a deity known as El, a sun god. Abraham's god was no longer specifically called a sun god, but his ascendance was a precursor to the adoption of exclusively solar values. When solar values were separated from lunar values, the solar ones became exaggerated and disconnected from the greater whole.

Everyone is a moon, and has a dark side which he never shows to anybody.
—Mark Twain

The solar side of consciousness is necessary for survival. No one can thrive without clarity and strength of purpose. The problem with solar domination is not that solar values are in themselves destructive, but they are at their best when they are balanced by lunar values. To meet any goal, the ability to connect with others is crucial.

Moreover, when the solar value system of rationality rejects the lunar value system of emotions, they do not really disappear, but reappear as negative projections. They are irrational and get projected onto other individuals or nations. This is common in families. Based on unconscious agendas, one family member is assigned the role of the shadow and represents a secret or denied side of the family history. For example, a young woman is accused of being too emotional by her rigid father. He represses his emotional side because of his discomfort with emotions. Another example is the college student who comes back from his first year at school with a few C's in addition to A's and B's. His alcoholic father chews him out as being lazy for not getting all A's, as he had done in high school, even though the father never graduated from high school, let alone continued on to college studies. Both fathers represent a solar orientation with their negative projections. This negative projection happens not only in families but culturally as well. In historical context between nations, demonization is often reciprocal. For centuries Islam has demonized Westerners, Jews and Christians; and Westerners, Jews and Christians have demonized Islam.

The story of Islam, like Judaism, began after Sarah gave birth to Isaac. The story illustrates how solar projections are not only an individual and family dynamic but are also a significant factor in the value systems of how cultures are organized. Power rather than love becomes the cultural driver. Instead of loving both sons, Isaac and Ishmael, Abraham and Sarah banished Ishmael to the wilderness.

Any archetypal motif like that of two brothers or twin heroes who have been separated into polar opposites, rather than held in complementarity, will evolve with each one taking a polar position. Judaism and Isaac claiming the solar individualist heroic pole leaves the lunar communal pole to be claimed by Ishmael and adopted by the Muslims and Muhammad. Judaism claims individual rights and private property, via the solar covenant from Yahweh. Muhammad's new religion moved to bolster itself by reviving communal values and tribal property via the lunar orientation with Ishmael.

Muhammad worshipped several gods, among them, "al-Lah" ("the God"), the highest god of the ancient Arabic pantheon. Many historians believe that this al-Lah was the same god who was earlier called "El" and later "Yahweh," and was first worshipped by Jews and then by Christians. It is significant that, as with the Hebrew god "El," Allah was also a solar god who dominated the other gods and goddesses in Muhammad's teachings. Worshipping one god brought a focal point to Muhammad's tribe, the Quraysh, as well as to other tribes in the region. Its focus settled violent quarrels and helped to unify them. As with the Hebrews, economic change was a major motive for unification. The shift from a nomadic life to one of a shared agricultural society helped bring about this change. The renowned ninth-century Arab Muslim poet and Muslim convert Abu Tamman describes:

> No, not for Paradise didst thou the nomad life forsake:
> Rather, I believe, it was thy yearning after bread and dates.

While Islam claimed the Muslim religion as the only authentic revelation of God, a drive to accumulate new territories and improve the tribes' economic condition began for them also. At the same time, consistent with the goal of creating an empire, there was a concomitant drive to bring Islam to all mankind. Eventually, both goals were pursued through military incursions that imposed Muslim beliefs by violence and domination. The same was true of Judaism, and later, Christianity.

Individualism, as we know it, emphasizing private property rights rather than the tribal group rights, arose among Hebrews with not only the advent of monotheism but also from Abraham's covenant with God. Individualism is a concept crucial to the modern ego. While the Muhammad solar god, "al-Lah" emphasized the lunar values of community rather than individualism, a personality profile was stamped into their collective psyche, which still rules thousands of years later. Virtually concurrent with the monotheistic Judeo or Judeo-Christian adoption of individual rights over group rights (a solar trait), Muslim monotheism was adopting the opposite, of group rights over the individual (a lunar trait).

The use of solar and lunar symbols emerges in the flags of Judaism and Islam, mirroring the archetypal aspects of each religion. The Jewish flag shows the six points of the Star of David (denoting a sun), and has no lunar symbols. This is pertinent when we remember that the Jewish religion does not allow any images (lunar) of God. The flag of Islam has a crescent moon representing communality, imagery and visual art and the star (sun) represents the warrior nature of Islam.

The psychological transformation from group to individual consciousness in Judeo monotheism constituted a significant shift that, with the ascendance of Roman Christian monotheistic influence, created Western culture. Before this time, individual fates were understood only as part of a larger story, as the history of a tribe or of a people. Just as property was held communally, each single fate was perceived as belonging to a larger web of connections throughout most of the world.

With the shift from polytheism to monotheism, the lunar vision of reality—a way of knowing bound to community and the earthly experience of life; one that valued relatedness and sensual knowledge—was sacrificed. This vision of the universe as an organic, sacred whole was replaced by fragmentation. Humanity became opposite to nature, to intellect, to emotion, to spirit, and to matter. Tribe set against tribe, and whole peoples were set in conflict.

The rejection of lunar values in Western tradition is not confined to the story of Abraham. Though Christianity began with a revival of lunar values, lunar consciousness soon diminished in this religion too. Despite the fact that Christ is called "The Prince of Peace," Christianity sacrificed the clear lunar teachings of Christ for another set of values. Within Christianity, a predisposition to war gained early ascendancy during the reign of the Roman emperor Constantine. The night before a major battle, in which his troops were outnumbered, Constantine was commanded in a dream to place the cross—the sign of Christ—on the shields of his soldiers. After winning the battle, Constantine attributed his victory to the power of "the God of the Christians." He converted to Christianity in 312 A.C.E. and committed himself to spreading the Christian faith from that day on. Though Constantine had previously persecuted Christians, Christianity was now tolerated throughout the Roman Empire, and eventually became the official religion of Rome. As a warrior for Christ, Constantine subsequently became the sole ruler of the eastern half of the Roman Empire.

Rather than advocating peace, Roman Christianity adapted itself to the ambitions of the empire. This was made easier by the dualism of spirit and matter, emotion and intellect, and solar and lunar values inherited from Judaism and Islam. Though our culture has been strongly influenced by this history, we do not have to continue to repeat it. If we reclaim our lunar resources, not only can we avoid self-destruction, we can be better able to address the very real threat that terrorists pose today. Just as the polarized twins project their characteristics on the other, culturally, we must embrace and thereby create balance better able to withstand and diffuse extremism on both sides.

For the next thousand years since Abraham, as the solar side of the psyche has become dominant, lunar perspective has become a secondary phenomenon. Judaism, Islam and Christianity were habitually demonized by the other. Today, our image of terrorists evokes this shadow land of lunar consciousness. From a solar perspective the lunar is mostly "loony" and "irrational." The acts of violence and impersonal madness of the terrorist fully reflect this lunar projection.

Yet to say that Western culture projects lunar traits onto Ishmael is not to imply that terrorists from the Middle East are lunar. We *project* the lunar onto them. Terrorist organizations are as solar-dominated as the American and European governments that battle them. In 1998, in an example of solar thinking, Osama bin Laden declared that his *jihad* was a "holy war" against the United States. He said that the "crimes and sins committed by the Americans are a clear declaration of war on God" which to him justified the bombing of U.S. Embassies in Africa and, eventually, the attacks on September 11, 2001.

The word *jihad*, "striving in the path of God," appears frequently in the Qu'ran. It is about an internal struggle for enlightenment, an interpretation that would signify the more lunar process of reflection. But the same phrase has been subverted recently, by fundamentalists, to mean an armed struggle for the advancement of Muslim power. In being appropriated by bin Laden, the meaning of *jihad* has been erased and reflective consciousness has been excluded from his program.

The fact that American culture has been dominated for centuries by a solar perspective has not escaped some of our finer writers. An eerie mirror of our contemporary condition can be found in the great American novel *Moby Dick*, by Herman Melville. It has been suggested that this work contains a reflection of the essential character of the American psyche. Even the first line of the novel, "Call me Ishmael," invokes the story of the two brothers in the Bible whose separation and subsequent enmity represent the deep split in our collective soul between the solar and the lunar.

One interpretation of Melville's first line, "Call me Ishmael," can be seen as what mythologist Joseph Campbell called *"the call to adventure of the archetypal hero's journey."* In the first stage, the initiate either attempts or refuses the call. Melville's call in *Moby Dick* reflects the call to America in its solar dominance to find, and then claim, the lunar half of itself for its own salvation. The story of *Moby Dick* shows the collective cost of trying to conquer the lunar twin.

Moby Dick was published in 1851. It recounts the tale of Captain Ahab, who lost his leg in an earlier encounter with the great white sperm whale called Moby Dick. The reader meets the vengeful and terror-provoking Captain Ahab several days after his ship, the *Pequod*, has sailed, as he walks broodingly back and forth on the deck. Assembling the entire ship's company, Ahab announces his mission to pursue and kill Moby Dick. Exercising a true monotheistic morality, he sees the whale as the embodiment of evil.

As the voyage continues and the ship encounters and kills other whales, Ahab's obsession to destroy Moby Dick becomes increasingly maniacal. When Moby Dick is finally sighted, harpoon boats are launched to kill him. The great white whale attacks Ahab's harpoon boat and destroys it, but Captain Ahab survives. The next day Moby Dick is again sighted, and again the boats are lowered. This time the great whale is harpooned, but once more Ahab's boat is destroyed, and one of the crew is trapped in the harpoon line and dragged overboard to his death. On the third day, the boats are sent once again, but this time Moby Dick rams the *Pequod* and sinks it. In the vortex of the whirlpool created by the sinking ship, Ahab is caught in his own harpoon line and hurled out of his boat to his death, just as the remaining members of his crew also drown. The sole exception is Ishmael, the teller of the tale, who was far enough away that he escaped death. Ahab's hero's journey fails because of his solar greed. Ishmael, with his lunar perspective, lives.

Looking at *Moby Dick* as an allegory, the central protagonists in the story—Ahab, Ishmael, and Moby Dick—can be read as symbolic figures who play out a profound conflict that lies at the deepest level of the American character. Evoking the rejected half of our collective soul, Ishmael, who carries the attitudes and values of "the outsider," tells us in the first paragraph that he is going to sea to escape a mood of suicidal depression which he describes as "damp, drizzly November in the soul." Thus the psychological starting point of the novel evokes not only watery, lunar realms but also the deep emotional despair that haunts the American psyche.

Just as the sea acts, in this novel, as a symbol for the collective unconscious, Moby Dick represents the primal energy of life within that territory. From this perspective, the wounded Ahab is attempting to kill a part of himself, his connection to, and reliance on, nature.

In this allegorical context, Ahab can be perceived as the solar hero. He is captain of the *Pequod*, which sails on Christmas Day. Ahab even speaks of himself as the sun's equal, "Talk not to me of blasphemy, man; I'd strike the sun if it insulted me." From this perspective, it is easy to see Moby Dick as a symbol for the psyche's lunar dimension, with which both Ahab and the American character are at war.

By understanding these allegorical meanings, Ahab's hunt for Moby Dick can be understood as a study in the psychology of solar hubris. While it was the solar side of his personality that helped Ahab develop the qualities needed to become the captain of a whaling ship, he suffers from the common flaw of most solar heroes, inflated pride. He believes that in his pursuit of Moby Dick he can enact his will and, like a monotheistic god, remain immune from the forces of nature.

Ahab's vow of vengeance mirrors the urge of a solar society to conquer and punish others in response to trauma. A chilling contemporary parallel to Ahab's obsessive response can be found in the Bush Administration's reckless crusade to stamp out all those who are perceived as "evil," even if there is no proof of their aiding terrorists or accumulating armaments. This response, Melville's narrative makes clear, is often self-destructive.

In the end, Melville's story does give us symbolic wholeness. Our last view of Ahab shows him being carried into the depths of the sea, tied to Moby Dick by his harpoon line, an image that reminds us of an umbilical cord. Thus, Ahab is finally reconnected with the watery, womb-like world of the lunar. Ahab cannot relinquish his addiction to solar dominance as he throws his harpoon a final time. "Thus, I give up the spear," he says as he dies.

We do not have to pursue annihilation. If we reclaim our lunar resources, not only can we avoid self-destruction, we will be better able to address the very real threat that terrorists pose today. With today's exclusive solar focus, however, we are not able to distinguish between defense and aggression, nor can we explore the full range of diplomatic solutions. Seeing aggression as the only workable response, we are setting in motion a cycle of violence that in the end will only increase the threat of terrorism.

Whether we are speaking of the war against terrorism or terrorism itself, the dilemma remains the same. Aggression leads to and creates greater and greater solar-lunar imbalances, which then lead to more violence. Through the prominence of military values and the idealization of the warrior, which always takes place during warfare, violence increases solar inflation. To resolve this conflict in other than militaristic ways will require all of us to elevate the lunar values of caring and relationship to equal the force of aggression as we respond to the war on terrorism.

There are pundits who would argue that both religion and psychology are irrelevant to the current crisis because the real issue is oil. These two explanations are not in conflict. The desire for dominion, which is driven by solar values, includes a drive for oil. Here we find an uncanny parallel between Ahab's hunting for whale oil, or spermaceti, one of the primary fuels of pre-industrial commerce, and America's garnering of petroleum from the Middle East. Yet the resource we most need for survival is not oil, nor does what we need have to be won in battle. Rather, it is something inside us that we need. We have become too dominated by solar values. Our society is in desperate need of lunar consciousness. One of the casualties of solar dominance is empathy, which is a lunar capacity. This loss has become apparent in our current policy toward Afghanistan as we abandon a people who, after enduring decades of Western and Soviet incursion and repeated warfare, including U.S. bombardment, remain in catastrophic circumstances.

In my work I have found empathy to be crucial in the healing of personal difficulties and conflicts in families. Often when clients feel besieged they are afraid, in the initial stages of recovery, to adopt empathy. They believe this will only weaken them further. Yet they soon learn that being empathic is not just turning the other cheek, nor does it make them passive victims. Feelings of empathy can, in fact, be independent of behavior. Indeed, empathic knowledge will make any defense far more effective. *The Art of War*, an ancient Chinese martial arts manual, recommends that when conflict starts, "knowing the other and knowing oneself" is the best position from which to respond.

Empathy is not simply a form of altruism. Because of its crucial role in learning it is also essential for survival. The tendency toward empathic imitation is hardwired into the brain and is, in fact, inseparable from the way that we learn. Empathy or "feeling into," the definition of the Greek word *empatheia,* is the first way we explore the experience of other people. An infant learns language, for instance, by mimicking adult sounds.

Empathy is also essential to the formation of the individual psyche. The authentic emotional self takes shape as a response to being cared for and loved; love and care by their very natures evoke love and caring for others. In turn, lack of empathy, often the result of trauma, causes severe problems. Criminal psychopaths, rapists, and child molesters, for example, have been discovered to have little or no empathy.

Emotional empathy goes beyond intellectual understanding. With intellectual understanding, though knowledge is grasped analytically, it is not always experienced emotionally. We may know how many children starve to death every day, for instance, but this is different from understanding what it feels like to suffer hunger as one of these children do, or what it is like, as a parent, to witness your child starving to death. Emotional understanding has profound consequences. It can transform intellectual knowledge. Empathy works a mysterious alchemy through which solutions emerge that may not have been visible before.

In my practice I have also often been called on to resolve dysfunctional behavior in businesses and corporations. Introducing empathy into a work place, whether a small business or a large one, radically improves not only the atmosphere, but everything from cooperation among employees to production.

Over and over again in international and ethnic conflicts, the interventions that have employed empathy have been surprisingly successful. Through the work of small non-government organizations in Nigeria, Ireland, and Israel, for instance, small accords have been accomplished. Think what might happen if these methods were to be used more often by governments. In our own recent history, citizen diplomacy with the former Soviet Union played a significant role in the end of the Cold War.

After World War II we developed vast international plans for financial aid such as the Marshall Plan, which gave aid to war-torn Europe. Despite the clear success of this approach, we appear to have learned little from this experiment. We have instead fallen back to an old paradigm, one that has been geopolitically dysfunctional for centuries. As Phillip Bobbitt, a former national security official in the Carter White House suggests, ". . . the most important single step that we could have taken . . . that we still need to take, is a change in mindset."

In the current international crisis, to put more cooperative strategies in place would require a quantum leap in consciousness. We will have to step out of our old mythology to embrace a new set of values. As radical as this shift may seem, empathy and all lunar modes of consciousness belong to a primal way of knowing and being that developed over the millennia as survival skills, long before language and other cognitive abilities had fully evolved. It is a way of knowledge that reflects the interconnectedness of all life.

This knowledge still exists in us, even if only on a cellular level. Lacking access to the lunar, we are like plants without roots. It is not just our current crisis that hangs in the balance. We must reclaim the full dimensionality of our consciousness if we are to achieve lasting peace, both inner and outer, and live harmoniously with the earth that sustains us.

CHAPTER SIX

Using *Solar Light, Lunar Light*

A Workbook

Whether we are raising children or making art, engaging in scholar-ship or business, everything we do in life requires both learning and practice. The same is true for psychological development. Indeed, the self is not simply born, it is created. Just as learning and practice are continuous processes in every other aspect of our lives, the self, too, is continually created and recreated throughout a lifetime.

Dynamic or adaptive change is a mandate of the soul. Those times in our lives when we feel less vital are often a result of resisting the continuous creative process that is our birthright. This application section is designed to help reclaim dynamic change in your life.

The first step on any path to healing or wholeness is self-under-standing. To begin using *Solar Light, Lunar Light* you must first deter-mine where your natural and developed tendencies are now; whether you tend to be more solar or more lunar oriented. The following guide should help you with that understanding.

Characterizations:

Most of us have learned and developed a "comfort zone" where we tend to "hang out" in our interactions and relationships. Barring a perceived need to change, we continue to use those elements, strate-gies, and behaviors that have worked for us in the past or that we are most comfortable with. A simple analogy is that most of us are either right-handed or left-handed dominant. Because we tend to use one more than the other it gets the majority of practice and thus we become more proficient with it. Being forced to switch and use the other for tasks requiring fine motor skills shows how much less developed it is.

Which tendency do you start with?

In the following chart, identity which traits best describe you. Use a score of 1 to 4 to describe how much of this trait you typically display:

1. Rarely
2. Sometimes
3. Often
4. Most of the time

Note: Identify how much you express each of these traits now, not how you did in the past, or how you want to in the future.

When you have finished, add up the scores in each column. Subtract the smaller from the larger. If your solar number was larger then chart the difference of the scores to the right of the midpoint. If your lunar score was larger chart the difference between the scores to the left of the midpoint. The position to the right or left of the midpoint tells you a relative tendency of being more solar than lunar, lunar than solar, or equally balanced solar and lunar traits.

The questions that follow may also help guide you in determining your orientation. Please remember that there are no right or wrong answers, this is simply a tool toward self-understanding.

1. What is the first thing you do in the morning if you are not rushed?
   a. Lie in bed and try to remember your dreams?
   b. Jump out of bed and get to the first task of the day?

	Lunar Traits		Solar Traits
___	Aware of Process	___	Analytical
___	Collegial	___	Assertive
___	Creative in the Arts	___	Clear
___	Empathic	___	Certain
___	Emotionally Aware	___	Creative in the Sciences
___	Flexible	___	Courageous
___	Intuitive	___	Decisive
___	Perceptive	___	Dominating
___	Relationship-oriented	___	Focused
___	Reflective	___	Results-oriented
___	Receptive	___	Precise
___	Sensual	___	Powerful
___	Sensitive	___	Responsive
___	Subtle	___	Task-oriented

50	40	30	20	10	midpoint	10	20	30	40	50
Strongly Lunar					Balanced or Versatile					Strongly Solar

2. If you wanted to consult a doctor or a lawyer, on what kind of information would you base your decision?

   a. Criteria such as where the lawyer earned their degree, what hospital in which the doctor practices, or information gleaned from the web?

   b. On your personal impressions after meeting the doctor or lawyer?

3. In your work, do you more often enjoy

   a. Planning and executing details?

   b. Spontaneous and creative tasks?

4. On a weekend or vacation, would you prefer

   a. Competitive activities

   B. Meandering walks?

5. Given a choice, would you decide to attend
   a. A lecture?
   b. An event at a museum or gallery?

Interpretation

1. If you jump out of bed to perform your first task, this is a more solar trait. If you prefer to linger in bed with your thoughts, this shows a more lunar tendency.

2. In choosing which professional to consult, if your decision is based on objective criteria, that method is solar. If you rely on personal impression, your choice is more lunar.

3. Planning and executing details is a solar choice, at least in the way you like to work. On the other hand, if you prefer spontaneity and creativity, your approach to work is more lunar.

4. Competitive activities appeal to the solar side of the psyche. Meandering walks are a favored lunar activity, allowing for a more reflection.

5. In general, lectures appeal more to the solar side of consciousness. Art exhibits, on the other hand, speak to us through sensual knowledge and are more lunar.

Clearly, if you have checked more solar than lunar traits, your approach to life is more heavily influenced by the solar than by the lunar, and vice versa.

Working towards Balance (wholeness)

Being predominantly solar or lunar does not necessarily mean you are out of balance. The following chart will help you determine if you are so. On the left, it lists characteristics of both solar and lunar dominance.

Being Out of Balance (either/or)		Achieving Balance	
If Solar Without Lunar	**If Lunar Without Solar**	**Solar**	**Lunar**
Ego Driven	Self Deprecating, Self Doubting	Confident (courage to enact ideas)	Willingness to admit limitations and mistakes
Dominating, disconnected or isolated from others	Appeasing others, not taking a stand for values	Strong convictions and willingness to take action	Cooperative, collaborative with others to achieve results
Abrasive Inflammatory	Lenient, lax	Responsible	Empathic
Obsessive and Compulsive	Lacking focus	Precise, diligent	Connecting the dots
Perfectionist	Lack of will	Desire to achieve, high standards	Willingness to fail, be vulnerable
Narrow Minded	Living in a fantasy world	Goal oriented	Visionary
Authoritarian	Follow the herd	Powerful	Compassionate
Rigid, not able to adapt	Aimless	Structured	Flexible
Cocky	Helpmate	Self Conviction	Receptivity

This chart can be used for growth as well as for evaluation. The first two columns under the heading "Being Out of Balance" lists traits that you may be experiencing as a result of either a solar or lunar dominance. The remaining two columns give suggestions for a change. Two parts of the suggestion:

a) Mellow your dominant strength or trait. For instance, if you are ego-driven, you can recognize the strength of this trait in solar column under achieving balance as confidence and courage to act. This is probably a strength of yours that you have overused to the point of being ego-driven. You will want to retain the strength and find other ways to express it.

b) Practice using the complementary behavior, which you will find in the complementary column under achieving balance. Using the same example of being ego-driven, you can explore the lunar complement which is the willingness to admit mistakes. Being willing to admit a mistake is often very difficult for solar driven people.

Of course, being willing to admit a mistake is easy to suggest, yet not so easy to achieve. Applying the information and balances in *Solar Light, Lunar Light* can help in this journey. Other traits in the lunar balance column are also helpful to acknowledge mistakes. The reason for a more forgiving lunar aspect of consciousness is that, one is less focused on individual performance in a lunar state. Performance from a lunar perspective emphasizes being one part of a vast whole. Seeing mistakes from a broader place makes them less personal and, ironically, easier to own. It becomes less important to defend your ego, and becomes easier to be more empathic.

Suppose, on the other hand, you favor the lunar side of consciousness. Occasionally a parent or teacher, for example, is too lenient with children. The way to balance this is not to become a disciplinarian. A strength of this lunar trait is that you probably have a lot of empathy with the children. You want to retain this, while not overusing it to the point of leniency. Developing out the complementary solar trait, under "Achieving Balance," harmonizes empathy with responsibility. Being responsible toward children means that you do not allow them to do things which are harmful to themselves or others. Learning responsibility will be easier for a lunar dominated person if other traits, such as self-confidence, are explored. Developing the confidence to trust your own judgment, for instance, will help you to hold the space for being less lenient when conditions call for it. The same would be true for the solar trait of precision. If you learn to measure and monitor, you will be able to exhibit more responsible behaviors because you will have better tools to monitor and measure.

Self Reflection

Keep a journal about experiences that are important to you. After you have journaled, go back and reflect on which mode of consciousness was active during each experience. If you used both modes, the solar and the lunar, note any subtle differences. Being aware of which mode of consciousness you use will help to further develop both aspects of your psyche and will present you with an alternative approach if the one you are using is not entirely successful or adequate.

Find a Role Model

Find a figure who inspires you in this particular trait or archetype. You might take notes of how this individual handles certain situations or how they express the qualities that you want to develop. When you find yourself in similar situations, you might imagine how they would react and try to emulate that. If this person is accessible and is willing to assist you, you might ask them to help you reflect on their perception of over-use or under-development of traits in particular situations or experiences where your strategies did not work as you would have liked.

Tapping the Energy of Complementarity

Now that you are becoming more aware of the modalities of consciousness, you can begin to be more creative with complementarity. When you have a problem, try switching the solar or lunar modality through which you are viewing it. This may help to find an alternative way to solve the problem.

Consider a specific difficulty in your life. How are you approaching to solve it? Through loosely articulated feelings and images (lunar), or analytically (solar)? Describe the same problem using the other modality. What new insights or feelings does this description give you?

If you are experiencing writer's block, for instance, determine whether you are working in a more solar or lunar fashion. The block may be eased if you shift from one mode of consciousness to the other, a solution you can continue to alternate each time you begin to get blocked.

Idealizations

Idealizations keep us from the deeper wells of creativity and keep us locked in our current modality. They are the expectations we place upon ourselves or others, or believe that others have placed upon us. They keep us imprisoned by false belief and criticism, denying access to our authenticity. Similar to unquestioned gender identifiers, idealizations do not have a basis in truth or reality, but in bias. The following exercise helps in getting to the core of where we might be stuck in resolving a particular issue. This exercise may seem very simple, but the effects of practicing it can be profound. Because the exercise helps deflate our bias, it taps into our unconscious—the voice of the authentic self. Once this voice or "inner knowing" becomes available to you, a greater and more spontaneous range of emotional responses will become apparent. Just as important, since our idealizations keep us locked in our primary modality, the habit of this exercise will begin the process of rebalancing.

Please be aware that some experiences are best identified and worked through with the help a trained professional. Please use common sense in the following through the information you receive from doing this exercise. The following is an example of which many people may be able to do on their own.

The Six Steps

Step One: Notice, and be empathic with any feeling you may have that is part of your mood now or is a habitually troublesome one that you would like to try to change, such as frustration, anger, sadness, or despair. Suppose, for example, that you have a general feeling of disappointment. Though you may not know why you have it, acknowledge and name it. Just naming it may help you to understand why you are disappointed. For example, you might realize you feel disappointed because you have not been promoted. With or without this new knowledge, proceed to Step Two.

Step Two: Ask yourself what idealizations (or expectations) may be creating your feelings. Negative feelings often occur because of the disparity between reality and our imagined fantasies: the authentic self and the imagined self. Because idealizations are so habitual, you may not see them as idealizations when starting to do these exercises. If this is the case, instead of trying to figure out what your idealization may be, allow yourself to free associate.

Relax. Sometimes it helps to shut your eyes and take a few deep breaths. Notice what comes to mind. It may be, for instance, the first line of a song, an image, or a simple wish. The unconscious mind usually offers what you need to know. Following our example again, after thinking of your disappointment, you may get an image of yourself as a company executive sitting in a large office at the top of your building.

Step Three: Imagine your idealization inside an inflated balloon—now pop it. You could write or draw the idealization on a piece of wood or paper—now throw it in an imaginary fire. It is important to use images with which you are comfortable as you access your unconscious and relinquish any attachments, some of which you may not even be aware. Thus, following our example, in your mind's eye you would place the image of being a company executive in a balloon and pop it, or throw it in a fire and see it burn up.

Step Four: Immediately after you have popped or burned the idealization, an image or thought will emerge intuitively. Wait for it without expectation of what it will be. Explore and reflect on the meaning of this image in your life. For example, after your idealization of being an executive vanishes, an image of playing with your children might flash into your mind. Gradually, you may become aware that in fact you were ambivalent all along about the promotion you didn't get, and you were worried that the obligations of this particular job might not allow you to spend the valued time with your family at this point in your life.

Step Five: Take action inspired by your new insight. In this example, you might talk with your spouse about how the promotion would have negatively affected your family relationships. Many programs for self-healing and growth recommend speaking frankly of new insights with a loved one or friend. Ask them to witness you as you move forward with an intent of acting on what you've discovered. For instance, you might begin to make practical plans for activities with your children, or to spend more time with your friends or spouse.

Step Six: Recognize how this particular idealization blocked your authenticity and creativity. Anything, including an insight reached by intuition, can evolve into an idealization once it becomes a rigid belief. Therefore, step seven is to continue to stay in touch with the voice of your authentic self. Repeating the first five steps can help you access full consciousness whenever you feel stuck.

FINAL SUMMARY

One of the meanings of emotional integrity is to feel whole. It is obvious that once you have reclaimed portions of your authentic self that were previously denied or repressed, you will begin to feel more complete. This integration will lead to a far richer inner life. You will then be living in emotional integrity.

Finally, you will also have a great deal more energy available with which to act on your new self-knowledge. This is true for many reasons, not the least of which is that you will be spending less energy in repression and denial. What is also true, is that you will be acting more in concert with your authentic desires.

This does not mean that your inner life loses its complexity. Self-knowledge seldom reveals a monochromatic, unified inner world. Most of us have ambivalence, if not contradictory wishes, desires, and thoughts. But with emotional integrity, if all of these aspects are recognized and acknowledged, they can be accepted in the same way that we accept the diversity of life forms. From this perspective, we can begin to understand the many aspects of our spirits and souls as a range of possibilities, a realm of potential outcomes.

As we begin to accept ourselves as complex beings with a widening range of responses, so do we begin to view others as possessing the same complex potential. More and more evidence is accruing toward the theory that not just human beings, but inanimate objects, systems, and the universe itself, is conscious. Whether or not that is so, the creativity of the universe is indisputable. The universe is constantly evolving both on planet earth and in the vast stretches of space around us. The fact that the continual creation of the self is natural to human nature reflects this changing nature and creativity of the universe.

In this regard, it is hardly coincidental that throughout the evolution of humankind we have looked to the sun and the moon to describe the territory of our souls. Indeed, where both the solar and lunar aspects of the psyche are developed and work together in complementarity, we feel whole. Our lives become resonant and harmonious with the fullness of a world defined so dramatically and completely by the warmth of the sun in daylight, and by the cool reflective light of the moon at night.

Advanced Work

If this has been helpful and you would like further insight, we suggest that you take the PACE Profile. Go to www.PaceProfile.com and map out your individual developmental archetype. This is based on the author's model of using the solar/lunar modalities complementing the four primary elements of motivation (Purpose, Action, Change and Empathy). We hope in the future to build out other developmental exercises on this site.

PACE PROFILE

Solar and lunar consciousnesses co-exist in all of us. We live on a planet where separate lights prevail at the different times we call day and night. Many of us today have come to think of consciousness as what happens when we "wake up." We think of consciousness as a tool to seize the day, concentrate our energies, and heat up our prospects. We do not recognize that this is how things look only when we privilege the sun to illuminate our lives. Artificial light has prolonged the experience of the day, which ends for many of us now, long after the sun has gone down, in the unreal blaze of television. Only when we dream do those of us with that mindset recover a lunar perspective. The PACE instrument attempts to restore that lost perspective by giving equal attention to the solar and lunar points of view in the handling of critical life issues—purpose, action, change, and empathy. All of these problems in daily living will look and be handled differently depending on whether they are seen in a solar or a lunar light. Answering the questions the PACE instrument poses to you is a way for you to discover how your capacity to deal with life will look when viewed alternatively in a solar and a lunar light. The PACE instrument will help you to see how close you have come, in the way you live, to realizing both perspectives.

No charge to take the PACE PROFILE at PACEPROFILE.COM

Howard Teich, Ph.D. is a psychologist and consultant who lives and works in San Francisco, California. In addition to his private psychology practice for over 40 years, he has taught at the University of California, the California Institute of Integral Studies, Sonoma State University, and the Esalen Institute. His writings have appeared in publications such as *Chrysalis, Parabola, San Francisco Jung Institute Journal*, and *Noetic Science Review*, and have been included in several anthologies, including *Use of Comparative Mythology: Essays on the Work of Joseph Campbell*. His seminal work defining solar and lunar psychology is described at length in John Beebe's book *Integrity in Depth*.

INDEX

Tamman, Abu 79
Tao 50
Taoism 8, 50
Tarot 39
terrorism 73, 74, 84
The Art of War 85
The Revelation of the Hidden 16,
        17, 20
Tibetan Book of the Dead 10
Twain, Mark 77
twin archetype 22
twin consciousness 5, 36, 51
twin heroes 18, 19, 22, 78
twin mythology 18, 19
twinning xvi

U

underworld xvi, 20, 23

V

vampire 30
van der Rohe, Ludwig Meis 53

W

Water Carrier 18, 20
Watson, James 51, 52
wave-particle 45
Western medicine 68
Wolf, Fred Alan 49
World War II 86

Z

Zeus 61, 69

CPSIA information can be obtained
at www.ICGtesting.com
Printed in the USA
FSOW01n1240050615
7684FS

9 781926 975054